MW01290653

Cousin Camp:

A GUIDE TO INTENTIONAL GRANDPARENTING

Ramona Roberson

Copyright © 2010 Ramona Roberson
All rights reserved.

ISBN: 1-4392-6226-8
ISBN-13: 9781439262269

DEDICATION

*I dedicate this book to my grandchildren who blessed me with the opportunity to experience something so wonderful I just had to share it with others. Thank you to Phil Hodges, who convinced me to put this book in print, and to Tom Hanlon, I couldn't have done this without you. **A very special thank you to my husband who gave me the encouragement and support to get the job done!***

PREFACE

As grandparents, we have it made. We get to enjoy our grandchildren, snuggle with them, take them to parks and zoos, go out for ice cream and pizza, read to them and play games with them, and do all sorts of fun things together.

And in spending time—quality time—with our grandkids, we also can pass down our legacies, beliefs, and heritage, help them be firmly rooted in our faith, and create memories that will last both our lifetimes and theirs.

In short, we have the opportunity to have a tremendous impact on our grandchildren. And the more intentional that impact is, the better off we—and our grandchildren—will be. We do make an impact whether we know it or not.

Cousin Camp: A Guide to Intentional Grandparenting, then, is for grandparents who want to make their impact intentional. And I'll show you how to do that, no matter your circumstances. You can transform the time you have with your grandkids into time that both you and your grandkids treasure.

Yes, we face many challenges in carving out quality time with our grandkids: geography, money, the busy-ness of life. Sometimes it seems that every day of a child's life is crammed full with activities in which they "must" be involved.

So carving out that quality time is not easy. I know that firsthand.

My husband Roger and I currently split our time between our homes in Wisconsin and Arizona. Our grandkids live in California, Colorado, and Maryland. Believe me, I know it isn't always easy getting together with the grandkids!

That's why we decided to become intentional about it—before the grandkids grew up, became too busy with friends and activities and interests, and their Nana and Papa were reserved for a couple of short, perfunctory visits each year.

Cousin Camp is based on an annual event in our family that goes by the same name. Each summer all the cousins (our grandkids) who are five years old or older stay with us for one week, apart from their moms and dads. Roger and I dreamt up Cousin Camp and got it rolling in 2001. It's been going strong ever since. I'll tell you how we got the camp going, how we operate it, and how you can build quality time with your grandchildren, whether you have a week or a weekend or just days here and there. (So, no, you don't have to plan an annual, weeklong event to build that quality time!)

Beyond that, this book offers you insight and encouragement about being intentional in your relationships with your grandchildren. It will help you plan your own "camp," your own time with your grandchildren. It will answer the *why* and the *how* questions about being intentional. (And yes, the *how* questions include a subcategory of *how on earth do you expect me to have the energy to do this?!*)

Along the way, I'll tell you about our experiences with Cousin Camp. But this book is not meant to be a vicarious experience; it's meant to point the way for you to deepen your impact and your relationships with your grandchildren. I truly believe that God gave Roger and me this idea for Cousin Camp—and the passion and energy to thrive while doing it each year. We've been greatly blessed through it, and we'd love nothing better than for you and your grandchildren to be next in line for those blessings.

INTRODUCTION

Roger and I were sitting at our kitchen table on a sunny July morning in our northern Wisconsin summer home when the conversation turned to—what else?—our grandkids. That year, 2000, three new granddaughters had made their entrance into this world, bringing our total of grandchildren to eight (we now have ten—to some, a number that describes perfection, but we're always ready for more!). I was telling Roger about friends of ours who had just taken their grandkids to Disney World.

"Don't you think it would be fun to take our grandkids on a trip?" I said as I poured myself some more coffee.

"Take 'em all to Disney World?" Roger replied. "You think we could survive *that?*"

"I don't know. I wasn't necessarily thinking Disney World."

Then Roger said something that to this day astounds me when I think of it. He said it clearly and confidently, as if he had been mulling it over for days or weeks, which he hadn't.

"I think we should start something called 'Cousin Camp,'" he said.

I looked at him curiously. "What do you mean, 'Cousin Camp'?"

"I mean let's get the grandkids out here each summer and spend a week with 'em. Without their parents. Just us, the kids, the lake, fishing, hanging out with the old folks."

The "old folks," I knew, meant us, but I let that slide as I was trying to digest what he said.

"They'd have a blast," he added, as if that sealed the deal.

I have to admit, my first thought was, *Yeah, they might have a blast—but would I survive? Would Cousin Camp be "one and done," and they'd bury me out back after I had died of a heart attack or some stress-related disease?*

Don't get me wrong: I *love* my grandchildren. And something about Roger's idea appealed to me immediately, because I *did* want to spend more time with them, to get to know them better and have them get to know their Papa and Nana better (as they called Roger and me).

But I also know my husband: He's a big-picture guy. He comes up with the grand ideas and then the details are carried out by others—in this case meaning, of course, yours truly.

I questioned how much "detail" help I would get from Roger. I pictured him slipping away, leaving me with all the grandkids. I saw chaos and pandemonium (even though my grandkids are, of course, angels). I felt my blood pressure rising. I heard the cries of homesick youngsters who had never spent time away from their parents. I saw the kids being bored or argumentative or disobedient or all of the above. I wondered if I would want to crawl under my bedcovers and not peep out until the camp was over. I felt the passage of time would somehow slow down during that "Cousin Camp" week, that each minute would tick by in about an hour's time. Or that the sun would simply stand still for a day, as it did in the Bible story of Joshua and the Israelites defeating the Amorites. (Or worse yet, that the sun wouldn't shine, and we'd be stuck in doors all week!) But I feared I would feel more like the Amorites and less like Joshua.

"You really think we can handle all eight grandkids?" I said dubiously, making sure I emphasized *we*.

"I didn't say all eight. I'm not changing any diapers, if that's what you're thinking."

Actually, had God spoken directly to Roger and said, "Roger, I want you to do one of two things for Me: Either build an immense ark and gather all the world's animals, two by two, or change diapers for a week," Roger wouldn't have hesitated. "I'm off to Home Depot, dear!" he would say.

"I think we would want to have a minimum age," I said. "I think they need to be five years old before they come to Cousin Camp." This made things seem a lot more manageable, because at the time only two of our eight grandchildren were close to being five.

Roger shrugged and nodded in approval as he sipped his coffee. "Fine by me."

He was convinced from the beginning that it was a good idea (of course, it *was* his idea, so I guess it didn't take much convincing).

I mulled it over for several months, loving it at times and thinking I was insane for considering it at other times. Roger kept reassuring me it would work, that "we" could do it. My understanding of "we" was "I" would do the work and "he" would pay for the airline tickets and be behind me (at times, *way* behind me), saying "You go, girl!" while he went off fishing by himself or golfing with his buddies.

But little by little the idea grew on me, and I was finally sold on Cousin Camp. That winter I called our daughters, Robyn and Rona, and told them about the idea of the camp. Rona's son, Max, turned five that December, and would thus be "eligible" for Cousin Camp; Robyn's daughter, Payton, would turn five the following March.

Robyn and Rona reacted much like I did: They liked the idea, with reservations. Yes, it sounded neat and fun. Yes, it made great sense for the cousins to spend time with one another and get to know each other—and their grandparents—better. Yes, Max and Payton (whom I made sure I never referred to as "guinea pigs") would have lots of fun at the lake. Yes, it might be nice to have a little break from the kids, and it would doubtless be a great learning experience for them.

Still, the kids had never been away from their parents for so long; indeed, in Max's case, he had never been away overnight from his parents. They might get homesick. They might misbehave. They might drive us crazy. And on and on.

But just as the idea grew on me, it grew on Robyn and Rona. They finally agreed that Cousin Camp would be a great thing to do, and they planned to send their two five-year-olds our way that next summer.

So that's *how* Cousin Camp started. Here's *why* we started it.

1. To spend more time with our grandkids.

In 2000, our grandkids were spread out across the country. They lived in California, Colorado, and Illinois. Roger and I were splitting our time between Wisconsin and Arizona. We saw our grandkids two or maybe three times a year, for short visits each time. The grandkids wouldn't really warm up to us on those visits until it was time for us to leave.

We wanted more for them, and we wanted, quite frankly, more for us. We wanted quality time with the grandkids.

Time is the most precious gift we can give to our grandchildren. We all know grandchildren who have been showered with money and material gifts from parents and grandparents, only to come out the worse for it. You can make more money, but you can't make more time. When you give your grandchildren your time, you are giving them a portion of your life; you are giving them yourself. Proverbs 11:25 tells us, "The one who blesses others is abundantly blessed; those who help others are helped." Cousin Camp helps us bless our grandchildren, and through it we are definitely blessed in return.

Cousin Camp ensures us that we will have a greater *quantity* of time as well. That quantity wasn't happening with our couple of short visits a year. We've found that quality time is much easier to create when we have more time with the grandkids.

2. To develop deeper relationships with our grandchildren.

Let's face it: As kids grow older, if they don't already have a solid relationship with grandparents, they aren't looking to start those relationships as they enter their adolescent years. By then, the kids will be more than busy with friends and activities. They're not about to make time for Grandma and Grandpa if they haven't already developed a good relationship.

I want my grandkids to really know me—not to just put a name to a face. I want to be real in their lives; I want us to create memories together. I want them to remember that they baked cookies with me, that we had tea parties and played board games and cards. I want them to remember how I did things and how I talked. In short, I want them to remember the real *me,* warts and all! These things will happen only through spending quality time together.

3. To help the cousins get to know each other better.

In addition to getting to know *us* better, we want our grandchildren to know *each other* better. This isn't easy when you're separated by states. Our week together each summer is the foundation for their relationships to blossom with each other.

4. To pass down family traditions.

In addition to intentionally spending quality time with our grandkids, Roger and I started Cousin Camp to build a sense of family tradition. Part of that tradition is spending time at the lake. Our children love their memories of summers at the lake, and we want our grandkids to love the lake and northern Wisconsin as much as we all do.

In spending a consolidated chunk of time with us each summer, our grandkids are gaining a true sense of who we are and what we value. And as this happens, we are passing on our legacy to them, our beliefs, our family history. We are supporting our own children's efforts as parents in grounding their kids in our faith. And in doing so, we can have not only a lasting impact on our grandkids, but an eternal impact.

5. Because (we admit it) we're selfish!

Ultimately, the reason we do Cousin Camp is because we're selfish! We love our grandkids, and we want to enjoy them while we can. And that's reason enough, isn't it?

CHAPTER 1:
Camp Planning Essentials

If you remember nothing else from this book, remember this: *be intentional about the time you spend with your grandchildren.* That doesn't mean you have to be inflexible and rigid. It means when you plan your time, you have the opportunity to shape and deepen your relationships with your grandkids.

That's the whole purpose of Cousin Camp.

Of course, there are plenty of other things that I hope you remember from this book, but the foundation for everything you do in your camp is being intentional.

The rest of this chapter will help you be intentional as you plan your camp.

.. .. ..

A weeklong camp works for us, and it works for our grandkids. But this is not an all-or-nothing situation. You certainly can create lasting memories and relationships with your grandchildren in shorter chunks of time. The *quantity* of time is not as important as the *quality* of time.

And it doesn't have to be a "cousin" camp (or even a "camp"). That's the title of this book because that's what Roger and I run. You can do this for one grandchild, or you can do it for a child you are formally or informally mentoring. And you can call it whatever you want.

Be thinking about what to do with your grandkids before they visit. If you see an activity book you can use, pick it up. Have your antennae up for things to do!

Make It Special

You might wonder why we call it a "camp." It makes sense for us, because we are doing this up in the Northwoods of Wisconsin, and the alliteration—"Cousin Camp"—sounds good. But more than that, it makes it special for the grandkids. There's something about giving it a name that makes it more exciting. "We're going to go visit Nana and Papa," doesn't sound nearly so fun as, "We're going to Cousin Camp!" It denotes the idea that this time is special, with planned activities that are geared toward them—and that's exactly what Cousin Camp is.

So no matter how long you spend with your grandkids in these planned times, give it a name—"Gram's Club," "Nana's Playtime," "Grandma's Girls" (if you have only granddaughters), "Gramp's Guys" (for boys), or whatever best fits you and your grandkids. It will make your grandkids feel like the time is special, that *they* are special. And they are!

You Can Do This Anywhere

The beauty of doing a "Cousin Camp"—or whatever you end up calling your own get-togethers—is that you can do it right where you are. (For simplicity's sake I'll keep referring to it as Cousin Camp; know that I am referring to whatever you decide to call your own special time with your grandchildren.) Take advantage of the resources around you, whether it's big city attractions such as museums and aquariums, small-town amusements such as miniature golf and bowling, or the serenity of the natural resources around you, such as forest preserves and lakes. And remember, the simplest pleasures are often the best. The times you spend at home with your grandkids are more often than not the times that they will remember.

Sometimes the simplest pleasures are the best. One of my favorite times is when we settle down after an activity and I read to my grandkids on our porch while they snack.

Shaping Your Camp

Plan a camp that works best for you and your grandchildren. That could be a weeklong camp, or it could be a day camp. Or a weekend or an afternoon or a once-a-month camp. Every situation is unique. Again, the focus is on making the time special for the grandchildren and making it quality time. The end result you want is a close relationship with your grandkids.

There are many ways to build those relationships. There is no one "right" type of camp—except, perhaps, the one that works best for you. This isn't a science. This is you creating memories. My intention is to challenge and encourage you to intentionally plan your time with your grandchildren, not to intimidate you into thinking there is only one way to do this.

As you think through the following issues, your own camp will begin to take shape.

What Do You Want to Get Out of Your Camp?

As I said a little earlier, if you get nothing else out of this book (and I hope you get *plenty* more!), please get *this* out of it: Be intentional about the time you spend with your grandkids. Know going in what you want to get out of it. The "We're going to spend time with Grandma and Grandpa" becomes transformed into "We're going to Cousin Camp!" through intentional planning.

Grandparents are often cast in the role of reliable (and free) babysitters. There's nothing wrong with helping out in this way. In fact, if this is your situation, make the most of it by making those times special. We have two choices: We can be reactive in our times with our grandkids, planning nothing and responding to our grandkids' whims when they come over; or we can be proactive, planning events and activities that will be fun, help them learn, and facilitate the bonding that takes place when they see we are actively engaged and are intentional about our relationship with them.

So, whatever your goals are—to build stronger relationships, create memories, or pass down family traditions and heritage— plan your time with the grandkids so that those goals will happen. Can those or similar goals happen on their own? Yes, to some degree. But not to the degree that occurs when you are intentional about making them happen.

Kids Are Thirsty for Love

Flowers gain nutrients from a variety of sources: sun, rain, and soil. The combination of nutrients helps flowers to grow, bloom, and flourish.

So it is with kids. They are nurtured first and foremost by their parents, but important nurturing comes from extended family and others as well. I've noticed that kids who receive adult love and attention beyond their immediate home are the ones who really blossom. As grandparents, we're in a perfect position to provide some of that all-important blooming love!

Do you remember the TV show *The Waltons*? That was a great example of multi-generational love and nurturing. The grandparents were an integral part of the family, interacting daily with the kids and passing down wisdom while loving each child individually and uniquely.

The love that your grandchildren receive beyond their parents' love reinforces that they are special. It also makes up for some of the "not now" or "just a minute" comments they get from parents who are busy. Vow never to make those types of comments during your camps. Give your grandchildren your undivided attention, and they will never forget it.

"Undivided attention" is not a euphemism for "spoil them." I am not advocating that we cater to their every whim and let them commandeer our houses as their "candy, junk food, and PlayStation haven." Far from it! Rather, I am suggesting that we provide appropriate activities, supervision, and love to help them grow.

What Can You Do Physically?

Plan within your limits. If you're in good physical health and shape, then plan those trail hikes or those forays to the tennis court at the park. If you don't have the energy or strength to do what you'd like to do with the grandkids, either switch the plans or enlist the help of a teenager.

We all have different levels of stamina (and it's all but assured that your grandkids' levels will be higher than yours). Kids are high energy. There's nothing wrong with reaching out for help. I can guarantee you if you have a teenager help you with an event or activity, the grandkids will not think less of you, and it won't diminish your impact on them. If anything, it will enhance your impact, because all your grandkids will remember is they had fun and you were there, even if you weren't taking an active part in it!

Once I stayed with four grandkids at their home by myself while their parents were in Hawaii on vacation. The eighteen-month-old had a bug. Sure enough, within three days, I had the worst flu I've had in thirty years. I felt so miserable I could barely crawl out of bed, and I cried, prayed for God's help, because I couldn't deal with caring for the kids when I was so sick.

Well, I survived, and so did they. But I vowed never again to babysit for an extended time without Roger. So keep in mind what you can do physically, and plan accordingly.

A tired grandparent becomes a grouchy grandparent. Mission defeated.

Home Field Advantage

It's an entirely different experience when you're babysitting in your grandchildren's home, as opposed to them coming to your house. Particularly if you're staying with them for an extended time, you're consumed with preparing meals, keeping up with laundry and dishes and schedules, and so on. You've stepped into the role of surrogate parent; you've lost your grandparenting rights at this point. You're on their turf. When I babysat for my grandkids while their parents were in Hawaii, I wondered why I wasn't enjoying it (even when I wasn't yet hit by the flu bug) as much as I enjoyed Cousin Camp. Then it dawned on me: the kids were in their home environment, and while they enjoyed having Nana babysit, it wasn't the same as them coming to our house with special activities planned for them.

How Much Money Do You Plan to Spend?

Notice I didn't say how much money can you *afford* to spend. The object is not to plan activities that cost a lot of money, as if the amount you spend is equivalent to how much you love your grandkids. Yes, if you can afford to and want to, you can take them to Disney World. But low-cost or no-cost activities in the kitchen, backyard, or park can be just as fun and memorable.

In fact, my grandkids and I have greatly enjoyed making homemade cards and gifts for people out of material we find around the house. Those cards and gifts are more personable and meaningful to the recipient because we're not just sharing a gift, we're sharing *us* in the gift.

The point is to figure out what types of activities you want to do and count the cost—or to structure your activities with a budget in mind. That way you won't be surprised, won't feel like you're being badgered into doing something (again, because of that intentional planning you're doing up front), and you can decide on how much you want to spend without consulting your grandkids.

There's something to be said about teaching a child that life isn't all about buying toys or materialism. Try to give every visit some take-home value, such as "a penny saved is a penny earned," or other words of wisdom.

What Are Your Surroundings?

Take advantage of the natural and manmade resources around you. Try to see your surroundings from the vantage point of your grandchildren. What interests them that is within walking or driving range? Remember, what might seem mundane to you could be exciting and meaningful to them.

I ask about your surroundings primarily to remind you to keep things simple. Planning for your camp doesn't have to be—*shouldn't* be—difficult or time-consuming. Use what's around you, keep it fun and easy, and enjoy your time with your grandkids.

How Old Are Your Grandkids?

You need to plan age-appropriate activities. What will enthrall a five-year-old could bore a ten-year-old to tears. If you're not sure what's age appropriate, your library should have books with age-appropriate activities for kids. Ask other grandmothers what works with their grandkids. On the Internet you can find activities for various ages. Also, watch the newspaper for local events that would interest your grandkids.

It's certainly easier to plan for children who are only a year or so apart in age. But if they stretch farther apart than that, you have to plan accordingly. For example, if you're having a coloring or art activity, you can do the same activity for different ages, but use more advanced materials for the older kids.

As I added grandkids to Cousin Camp, the age difference grew to be five years. At that point I began buying workbooks with lesson sheets in them for the appropriate ages.

The main point is to be looking for activities that will be fun and engaging for each grandchild, and that tie in to your overall purpose for doing the activities.

How Many Grandkids Will Attend Your Camp?

Just as you have to plan for the ages of your grandchildren, you have to plan for how many you will be hosting. If you have two or three kids close in age, you can probably do the camp yourself (if you're young at heart and in good health—but above all, consider your physical abilities). If you have more kids, or if they are spread out in age, consider getting some teenage help. It never hurts to have an extra set of hands, feet, and eyes to help with crafts and other activities and to supervise for safety. By having the help, this frees you up to spend more time with your grandkids. For example, the teen can help by running errands, helping with meals, and so on—allowing you to focus more on the kids. Just be sure, of course, to get helpers whom you know you can trust.

*Don't be a hero!
If you need help because
of the number of grandkids you
have, get it. It will make your life
easier, and the kids will like
having a teen around.*

How Long Will Your Grandkids Be at Your Camp?

If you have your grandchildren for an afternoon, you just have to plan for a few hours together. If you have them for a weekend or longer, you need to plan more extensively.

For longer stays, it helps to have a routine in place. I'll talk about routines in the next chapter.

Do You Have a Special-Needs Grandchild?

If you have a special needs child, you need to determine if you can meet those needs or if you need help in meeting them. If your grandchild is limited physically, mentally, behaviorally, or in any other way, you will need to plan activities accordingly. There are numerous resources in libraries and on the Internet that provide activities for special-needs children.

What Are Your Mutual Interests?

The ideal is to plan activities that will interest both you and your grandchildren. A word to the wise here: Go with your strengths. If you're artistic, do artsy things with your grandkids. If you're a nature lover, get your grandkids out in nature and teach them about plants and trees and let them enjoy the great outdoors. If you're *not* an outdoors person, planting a flower garden will likely prove futile. The kids will sense your frustration, and your focus might be more on making those flowers grow (if by nothing else, by your sheer willpower and your threatening looks), rather than on the kids.

So do yourself—and them—a favor and stay away from things that hold no interest for you or for which you have little aptitude. Remember that most young grandkids will enjoy just about anything. They understand that it's about the relationship, not the activity—usually better than we do. (Have you ever been doing something with your grandchildren and realized that they are focused more on you than on the activity? Or that a granddaughter was stroking your arm or fingering your hair? Our first reaction often is impatience or annoyance, and we tell them to pay attention or get back to the task. By doing so, we interrupt a Kodak moment in the child's mind.) If you are doing something that you enjoy, chances are great that young grandchildren will enjoy it, too, whether you're finger painting, flying a kite, or playing a board game.

It does get a little trickier with older grandkids. They have more developed interests and are at a stage in life where they can be easily bored (and not afraid to express it). Don't let this frighten you off. Just consider how you can play to their interests, even if those interests aren't your forte.

For example, say you have a fourteen-year-old grandson who is really into planes and flying. And let's say you don't have either a pilot's license or the slightest interest in, or knowledge of, planes. What can you do?

You can take your grandson to a flight museum. Or get some books on flight from the library. Or take him to an airport to watch planes take off and land (or even to a private airport to meet and talk with some pilots). Or rent movies in which flight plays a central part or theme. Or have him work on a model airplane. Or take him to a park where he can fly his radio-controlled plane. Or…

You get the picture. Even if you're not an expert in one of your grandchild's areas of interest, you *can* think of things to do that would be fun for him or her. So put your thinking cap on and plan something that will make the visit memorable and fun!

Seeing Through the Eyes of a Child

When you're planning activities for your grandchildren, try to see the world through their eyes. What would a boy or girl who is five or ten or fifteen years old see? What interests a five- or ten- or fifteen-year-old child—not just *any* five- or ten- or fifteen-year-old, but *your* five- or ten- or fifteen-year-old?

If you think about it, you can make anything exciting—and a teaching opportunity. Many things that seem mundane to us are far from mundane to them. The younger ones especially are in a constant learning mode. Encourage that learning, growth, and exploration by doing things that excite them, invigorate them, and are simply—to a five- or ten- or fifteen-year-old—downright fun. Doing so helps the bonding process.

The best way to do this is to get into their world and see through their eyes. And when you do, what has been mundane to you might take on a new appeal!

What Does Everyone Want Out of the Camp?

There are three parties to consider here: your own children, your grandchildren, and you.

Parents

Many parents appreciate the break from their kids, even if it's just for an afternoon so they can get errands done or enjoy a nice, quiet lunch and some time alone. On the other extreme, shipping the kids off to the grandparents can allow the parents to take a vacation alone. This extended time can be wonderfully refreshing and recharging for the parents and a time for the grandparents and grandkids to bond—which typically is another ideal parents have for their children.

Sometimes parents think they have to be supermoms and superdads, providing perfect care for their children 24/7, never taking a break. The reality is that a break does them good and does the kids and the grandparents good as well. If you have children who you know are stressed and could use a helping hand but have difficulty in letting go, encourage them to try just a short trip—a weekend—leaving the kids with you. Chances are great that they will love it, and the grandkids will, too.

Absence really does make the heart grow fonder. A few days at your house will do wonders for your relationship with your grandkids—and they'll be eager to see Mom and Dad when they get home. No matter how good the visit is, everyone is ready to get back to normal at the end of the visit.

Kids

The inalienable right to have fun has been wired into every kid since the beginning of time. Your grandkids want to have fun with you, and they want the time with you to be special—your time together. What makes it special is it can't be duplicated somewhere else or by someone else; it can only be found at your house or with you. That's what they want, and that's what should guide all your planning efforts.

Last But Not Least: *You*

Perhaps your answer to what you want out of the camp goes something like this: "I want to bond with my grandkids. I want to draw closer to them, to get to know them better, to get to know them beyond the superficial levels. I want to learn to appreciate their distinctions and unique qualities, their strengths and weaknesses, their likes and dislikes, and everything that is in them that makes them who they are.

"And I want them to know *me* better. I'm not just a cookie-maker and treat-dispenser, and I'm not just an older, more worn out version of their parents. I'm unique and distinct in my own right, and have my own dreams and hopes, my own fears and weaknesses, my own passions and eccentricities (I prefer to call them strengths). And I have some wisdom and experience that can benefit my grandchildren, wisdom and experience that my grandkids' parents do not possess. So I am valuable to my grandkids, and they are valuable to me. And I want to make the most of my time with them, both to their benefit and to my own. Just as I want to know the real them, I want them to know the real me—and love me regardless. Just as I will love them regardless."

That might not be your answer word for word, but doubtless it hit a few themes that are important to you and drove you to read this book. We live in such a fast-paced society with families spread across the state or the country—even with in-town or close families sometimes so busy that they have difficulty scheduling time to see each other. Grandma and Grandpa often get shunted aside to holidays and birthdays. The relationships between grandparent and grandchild don't move past superficial or shallow.

Time, effort, love, and sacrifice are the antidotes to such relationships. If you want a deeper relationship with your grandkids, it's up to you to forge it. Don't expect it to happen on its own. You need to take the time to plan meaningful visits with your grandkids, and you need to take the time to make those visits happen. Your effort, love, and sacrifice are what make the camp happen.

Yes, it would be easier to kick your feet up, turn on the television, or go out to lunch with friends. But whatever you sacrifice in terms of your time and energy are more than worth it. You will get what you want: a close, lasting relationship with your grandchildren.

What more could you ask for out of your camp?

Time, effort, love, and sacrifice are the pillars of strong relationships. If you want a deeper relationship with your grandkids, it's up to you to forge it.

WHEN YOU KNOW YOUR CAMP IS SUCCESSFUL

When my grandson Max was ten, he had three five-year-olds, both siblings and cousins, joining him for the first time in Cousin Camp. I thought maybe Max and Payton, who was also ten, might enjoy attending sports camps in the area, rather than hanging out with several five-year-olds. (I was also feeling the pressure of entertaining multiple ages at the same time; I was being challenged and looking for an easy way out.) Max overheard me talking about this to his mom. He said, "Hey, Nana, why would I want to do that? I like *your* camp." In other words, "Just figure it out Nana, I'm coming back!"

When you get the stamp of approval from your grandchildren, you know your camp is working. His comment was all the encouragement I needed to dig my heels in and figure out how to handle camp for all the kids.

Setting Your Camp Theme

I highly recommend choosing a theme for each camp, because it gets the creative juices flowing. With a theme, the food, decorations, clothes, games, videos, stories, etc., all fall into place. Kids get into a theme; they love being creative and exercising their imaginations. Here are some of the themes we've used over the years.

CHRISTMAS IN JULY
Our focus that year was on the true meaning of Christmas, keeping in mind that the holiday is really about Jesus' birthday. So our finale was a birthday party for Jesus, complete with a cake and gifts for Jesus.

Crafts:
Set up an artificial Christmas tree and make tree decorations, such as glitter-decorated pinecones, or individual pictures glued to jar lids and trimmed with rickrack and ribbons. This is an easy one, as there must be hundreds of children's tree ornament ideas! Make crafts to give to each other for a gift exchange

between the kids. They love wrapping them and placing them under the tree.

Critter Christmas Tree:
Trim a small outdoor pine tree (or set out a fake tree) trimmed with pinecones smeared with peanut butter and rolled in bird seed, or decked with popcorn garlands or berry garlands— anything that birds and squirrels love to eat. Place the tree where you and the children can easily see it from inside the house. They'll love seeing all the critter activity!

Videos and music:
Kids love watching the Christmas stories and singing Christmas songs in the middle of summer.

Food:
Make and decorate sugar cookies, candy canes, and a birthday cake for Jesus (see "Jesus' Birthday Cake" under recipes in appendix b).

LIVING ON A SPACE STATION
Turn your house into a make-believe space station by hanging a sign above each door denoting a space station term (mission control center, welcome center, tech-lab, robot room). Disco balls, black lights, beads hanging in the doorways all add to the space feel. Think 70's.

We also made up special names for ourselves, using astronomical terms (Super Stars, Computer Geeks, Flying Cows-it's true!) Children love make-believe and it does not take long for them to get in the spirit of the theme.

Crafts included anything airplanes or stars, sun or moon. If you like playing background music during that time, the James Bond theme works well. With a little creativity, almost any food can be renamed something that denotes a space theme. Remember that all space food is dried or packaged in a form of plastic bag, zip lock sandwich bags. (see "Omelets in a Bag" in Appendix B) Also, a star-shaped cookie cutter can transform almost any item of food.

ROUGHING IT IN THE GREAT OUTDOORS

This one was easy even for me, who claims no creative abilities. Just think camping out/picnics...red-checked tablecloths, campfires, trees, squirrels and hiking boots. You are the Forest Ranger or Nature Guide. The children become scouts. Everyone is issued a bandana to wear around their neck. Warning...my kid's bandanas were worn everywhere from head to arms to ankles. But I loved the fact that they kept finding new ways to wear them.

Special Needs Children

This is of a more serious nature, but it sure captured their attention. Wanting to educate and expose my grandchildren to the reality of life with a child who has special needs, I went searching and discovered a wonderful five-day program just for this purpose. It was very informative and presented in a friendly, compelling way. My grandchildren were captivated and excited to discuss the different illnesses and share some of the experiences they have had with friends who have special needs. I thought of this program as an investment into my grandchildren's' lives. Hopefully, sometime in the future, I will hear how that information effected the way one of them reacted in a given situation. Then I will know that my original purpose had been accomplished...to make my grandchildren thoughtful, compassionate, and not intimidated when they come in contact with a person with a disability. I pray that they will be the ones who reach out in kindness, rather than the normal childhood mean-spiritedness.

The website for special needs is
www.joniandfriends.org

Other websites I use to find materials are:
www.cemlife.com
www.GuildcraftInc.com
www.ssww.com
www.gospellightvbs.com

SETTING THE THEME

Every year I buy inexpensive T-shirts and have the date or theme of our camp imprinted on them. I send them to the children a week or two before camp starts, to build excitement and anticipation. Don't send them too far ahead, or the excitement will die (or they might lose the shirts before they pack!). Sometimes I encourage them to wear their shirts when they travel, telling them it will help Nana recognize them when they get off the airplane. It also creates conversations for the kids as they travel, as people ask them about their "Cousin Camp" shirts. Of course, the main objective is to get a group picture in their shirts. We now have eight group pictures in matching shirts!

One year, I had a four-year-old granddaughter who was a younger sibling to three campers. When I was packaging up the camp T-shirts to send to the older siblings, it occurred to me that the little one might feel left out when the package arrived. So, running out to Wal-Mart, I grabbed a tiny white T-shirt and went to my computer and printed off an iron-on sign that said "Cousin Camp Wannabee." My daughter told me it was a stroke of genius. The little one would have been crushed if there had not been a shirt for her. And everyone had a good laugh about the imprint.

Parental Involvement

Cousin Camp is for you and your grandchildren; that's where the focus is. But obviously parents play a role in the camp, too. A question I often get is, "How involved should parents be?"

My answer is they should play a supportive, behind-the-scenes role. In my experience, the less direct parental involvement, the better. This is not an insult to the parents of my grandchildren; it's a reflection on the purpose of the camp, which is to deepen the grandparent-grandchild relationship. I've also noticed that kids seem to behave better when their parents are not around. Sounds strange, but it's true. When parents are around, kids feel freer to complain and whine and misbehave than when the parents are gone and I'm in charge. They're on their best behavior for me.

How can parents play a supportive role? Here are four ways:

1. **Parents can talk enthusiastically about the camp that's coming up. This is especially helpful for first-time campers and those who have not been away from home before (if they are staying one or more nights with you).**

2. **Parents can focus on the positives of camp. (Yes, there are negatives, at least at my Cousin Camp: When you get eight or nine siblings and cousins together for a week, there are bound to be some disagreements and hurt feelings.) So, rather than explore the argument a child had with a cousin, a parent can redirect the focus on the fun the child is having with other children there—or even with the cousin with whom he argued.**

3. **Parents should disappear once the kids are dropped off. When parents hover nearby, it distracts the kids and takes away from the time you have with them. It also puts the kids in a nether world: Is this Mom's territory or Nana's? When parents disappear, it establishes who's in charge.**

4. **Parents should respect camp guidelines. This is most applicable for weeklong camps. If you are planning an extended camp for the first time, parents might have concerns about their child being separated from them for days at a time. Talk through the issues with them, explain what you have planned, and assure them that their child will be safe with you and that you'll do all within your power to make the time fun and meaningful for the child. See the following letter for an example of the guidelines I'm talking about.**

Parent Letter

I write a letter each year to my grandkids before Cousin Camp begins. It helps prepare them—and their parents—for the camp experience. Here's my letter from a recent year:

July 16, 2006

Dear Campers:

It's almost camp time again, and Nana and Papa can hardly wait. We hope you are as excited as we are. Amanda and Luke are looking forward to being our counselors again this year.

Here are some reminders for you:

Tell your mom and dad that you will be calling home on Wednesday afternoon, around 5:00 p.m. their time.

Packing: please put your name on all your clothes so we don't get confused, especially when Nana does the laundry.

What to pack:
    1 underwear and 1 pair of socks for each day
    2 pajamas
    2 swimsuits
    3 short outfits
    2 jeans/long pants
    2 long-sleeved shirts
    1 sweatshirt or jacket
    1 pair play shoes
    1 pair good shoes/sandals
    1 pair water slippers, if you have them

Do not bring treats (except for a snack on the plane), money, or sports equipment. You can bring a favorite stuffed animal or doll (Lauren, Haley, and Jordan might want to bring their Hopscotch Hill dolls?).

If you have any questions, please call Nana. Have a safe trip and we'll see you soon!

Love,
Nana

Camp Cornerstones

At the beginning of this chapter I compared being intentional in planning your time to laying a foundation. Intentional planning sets the stage for a great camp, a great time with your grandkids.

I have another construction analogy for being intentional. I see it as one of four cornerstones that will help you plan and run a solid camp. The four cornerstones (or, the "Four Bs," if you will) are:

Be intentional.
Plan your time and activities with the end result in mind.

Be committed.
Commit to your plan—and to your grandkids.

Be creative.
Think outside the box. Don't settle for the "same old, same old." Try new things that challenge the kids, or try old things in new ways.

Be flexible.
Planning: yes. Being rigid about sticking to the plan no matter what: no. Learn to keep a good flow going even if that means changing plans.

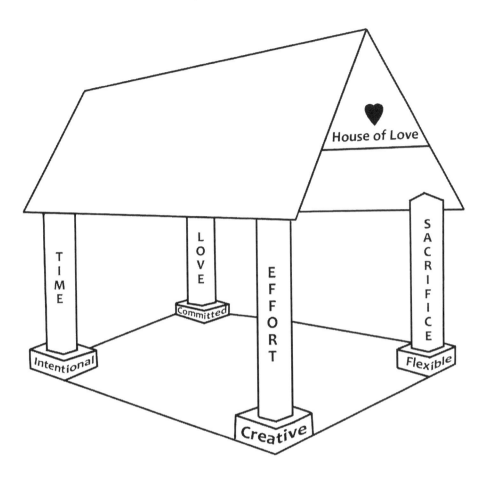

When you combine these four cornerstones with the four pillars I mentioned earlier in the chapter—time, effort, love, and sacrifice—then you are on your way to building solid relationships with your grandchildren that can stand the test of time.

You learned about the first cornerstone—being intentional—in this chapter. In the remaining chapters you'll learn about the other three cornerstones.

CHAPTER 2:

I can hear you now: "Routines and rules? Do we need to go that far?"

In a word: Yes. (But don't panic. If you stick with me here, you'll thank me in the end. I promise.)

If planning is the foundation for your camp, and the four cornerstones are "be intentional, be committed, be creative, and be flexible," then routines and rules are the mortar that will hold the bricks of your camp walls together. Or, consider them life jackets that can save you and your grandkids. Or, a rudder on your boat that can steer you home. Or, the gravity that keeps your grandkids' feet planted on *terra firma*.

However you consider routines and rules, consider them important. They make life simpler and more pleasant, and they provide a structure for your camp that will help it run more smoothly and effectively.

The longer your camp is—and the more kids you have—the more important routines and rules become.

Camp Routines

Routines bring balance to our days. Many people use routines without even realizing it. We who are retired might get up around the same time each day, have our coffee, read the paper or watch a morning news show, do some household chores, run an errand, have lunch, and so on. The day unfolds and there is variety in each day, but there is also some sort of loose routine that we follow. These routines are ingrained in us so much that we don't think about them; they just provide structure to our day.

The routines for working moms and dads are generally more rigid and evident, with work and kids' schedules for school, sports, music, and other activities taking up their days.

I see camp routines—at least for camps that are a full day or longer—as somewhere in between these two examples. The kids understand there is a structure to the day; it's not just a willy-nilly free-for-all all day long. But that structure is not so rigid or unyielding that it can't change, and it is not the end-all that must be followed, no matter what. Not with our "be flexible" cornerstone in place!

Learning Manners While Eating Lunch

I often read tidbits from a "manners for children" book during lunch, and we discuss manners afterward. The kids learn about manners (reinforcing what they learn at home, of course), and Roger and I have seen them put forth their best manners when we go out to eat.

The kids get a kick out of correcting each other regarding the proper placement of a fork or knife. It's fun with a purpose, because the bottom line is they are learning good table manners.

When to Use Routines

You can probably guess my answer here, but I'll say it anyway: *Use routines whenever you have your grandkids over.* That makes it simple, doesn't it?

How much structure you need depends on three things:
- How long will your camp last?
- How many grandkids will be with you?
- Are your grandkids hyperactive or do they have behavior or discipline problems?

Let's take these questions one at a time.

Length of Camp

If you're having your grandkids over for an afternoon, you don't need a lot of structure. You still want to plan the time, mixing in physical activities that help them blow off steam with sedentary or quieter activities. But it should be pretty simple to cover a few hours and shouldn't require too much planning.

However, if you're having your grandkids for an entire day, or for multiple days, you will help yourself by plotting out the time hour by hour. Yes, you can change that schedule. But it's important to have a schedule in place to change (or simply to follow). I've found that my grandkids actually like having a schedule, and they like to see the schedule, so I post the day's activities on my refrigerator in the morning. They cluster around and examine it, and they get excited about what they see coming up. A little later in this chapter I'll share a sample daily schedule.

Number of Kids

More kids equals more structure. This is particularly true if you have grandkids whose range in age requires activities at different levels. If you have a small army invading your house (and I mean that in the most affectionate way), you have to be prepared for that army. Otherwise chaos can result.

It gets down to who is in charge. *You* are in charge, and you want to keep it that way! Structure will help you do so. Structure says to the grandkids, "There is a plan in place, and Grandma's in charge of that plan." The kids' typical response to that is, "That's cool. Let's follow that plan and have fun!"

Hyperactivity and Other Behavior Issues

If you have a hyperactive grandchild, whether he or she is diagnosed with Attention Deficit Hyperactivity Disorder (ADHD) or not, having a structured day will help. Most kids' attention spans are not long, so having a plan to keep them interested, having fun, and active (not meaning "bouncing off the wall" active, but a controlled active) does wonders for making the time enjoyable.

The same goes for children who have other behavior issues as well. When kids are (a) on task and (b) having fun, then there is little time or inclination to be either intentionally or unintentionally disruptive.

Structure isn't meant to "clamp down" on kids. Quite the reverse: It's meant to free them up to have the most fun possible!

Using a Balance of Physical and Quieter Activities

Balance physical activities with quieter activities, such as reading or arts and crafts. Quiet time can also include quiet playing inside, with you nearby but not engaged directly in the playing.

Most of all, focus on your grandchildren when you are creating a schedule. Set up something that works best for them. If your granddaughter is a morning person, then schedule something active early on. If she wakes up slowly, let her do that, scheduling quieter activities to begin the day.

In other words, there is no one set routine that works for everyone. It's up to you to decide what works best for you and your grandchildren. Just make sure you find a good balance between physical activities and quieter activities.

Straying from Routines

In school, kids have routines—math at 8:30, geography at 9:15, and so on—from which they rarely stray. But even in school, they do stray from their routines on special occasions—for assemblies, special performances or visitors, and other events that take precedence over their normal schedules.

If it's okay to stray from routines in what is normally viewed as a rigid setting—school—then it is certainly okay to change the routine at Grandma's house. Here are just a few reasons to move away from your schedule and do something other than planned:

- The kids' energy is lagging, and instead of doing a physical activity they need some down time.
- The kids are bursting with energy, and the quiet activity you have planned isn't going to work very well.
- You or one of your grandchildren are ill, and you need to tone down all activities.
- Tempers have flared among the grandchildren, and one or more kids need a timeout.
- A child has a minor injury and needs a Band-Aid, a hug, and some quiet time to recover.
- The teen who had planned to help you with an event cannot make it for some reason.

- Bad weather preempts the outdoor activities that you had planned.

The key is for you to be aware of when these times come up, and not be so rigid that you can't change. Again, it's not about the routine; it's about the children. The routine is only there to facilitate the time you have together, to shape a day that is filled with fun and that draws you and your grandkids closer. So don't be afraid to change your routine. Just focus on changing it for the better.

Don't etch your schedule in stone. Create one—and then alter it as the need arises.

Sample Daily Schedule

Here's a sample day in our week at Cousin Camp. After this schedule, I'll talk about creating your own schedules. Check out Appendix A for menu ideas, Appendix B for a sample menu form, and Appendix B for specific recipe ideas.

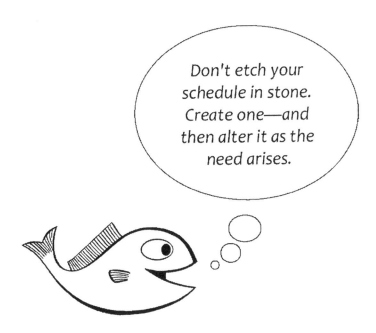

Don't etch your schedule in stone. Create one—and then alter it as the need arises.

COUSIN CAMP 2007
June 25–29

(Bolded items denote physical activities; the rest are quieter activities. Note the mix throughout the day.)

Daily schedule:

8:00—Wake-up call
        Breakfast
9:00—Cleanup time
9:15—Opening Assembly (theme presentation)
9:30—Music Time
10:00—Bible Stories
10:30—Activities
11:00—Craft time
12:00—Lunch
1:00—Water activities
3:00—Canteen and story time
3:30—Videos and free time
5:30—Dinner
6:00—Games
8:00—Baths
8:30—Snack
8:45—Bedtime stories
9:30—Bedtime
10:00—Lights out

Creating Your Own Schedules

So you've seen one day in the life of my camp. Do you need to stick precisely to that type of schedule? No. Construct what will work best for you and your grandkids. Prepare a schedule, yes, but be flexible. The kids will keep you on track.

Do note the ebb and flow in my schedule from being physically active to quieter activities, from being outdoors to indoors, from one activity to another. A schedule that keeps kids interested and is attuned to their needs—sometimes they need some down time, sometimes they need to burn off energy—is the ideal.

In the next chapter I'll share ideas for specific activities in a variety of areas. For now, keep in mind the importance of the ebb and flow of the day, of moving from active to quiet to active again, and of monitoring the energy levels of the kids to know when it is best to shift to another activity.

Post your schedule on the refrigerator or a wall. Kids love seeing schedules—they enjoy the structure!

Camp Rules

No, this is not Boot Camp; it's Cousin Camp. But rules among siblings and cousins are, I have found, highly useful.

Rules provide boundaries to protect kids physically, emotionally, psychologically, and spiritually. Smaller children need smaller boundaries, meaning you have a tighter rein on them, and bigger kids need bigger boundaries, meaning they get more responsibility, leeway, and privileges as they get older and show they can handle those bigger boundaries.

Rules also can simply make life more pleasant. They can take the person out of the equation. It's no longer an issue because your granddaughter leaves her clothes in the floor; it's a house rule that everyone understands. The rule is focused on the clothes, not the child. I've found that when my grandkids know the rules, they tend to keep each other in check. I don't have to police them on it.

One rule I have is regarding electronics: I make the kids hand over all iPods, cell phones, video games, and any other electronic technology once they cross our threshold. The whole point of our camp is to engage each other—to talk, to play, to learn, to have fun, to discover things together.

So I put the electronic equipment—along with whatever gum, candy, and money they brought—into separate zip lock bags and stash the bags in my closet. By the time their parents come to pick them up, the kids forget that they brought their electronics with them—because we've been having too much fun together.

DELEGATING RESPONSIBILITY TO JUNIOR COUNSELORS

When my grandkids Max and Payton turned twelve, I promoted them to junior counselors for Cousin Camp. As junior counselors, they had more responsibility in helping me make the camp run smoothly. They liked the idea—and so did the younger kids.

I got the younger kids to buy into this idea by asking them at the end of the previous Cousin Camp who would make the best junior counselors (I also asked them who was the neatest camper that year, the funniest, etc.). The kids voted, and it was an even split between Max and Payton. So going into the next camp, everyone was aware of the new situation and approved of it—as did I!

Addressing the Troops

Let your grandkids know up front that you have rules they need to follow, and if they break them, there will be consequences. I post rules on the first morning, right beside the camp schedule. I show them the rules and we talk them over—including the consequences for breaking the rules, such as timeouts, loss of participation in a game or activity, and so on—before we get going.

This next Cousin Camp I'm going to get the kids' input on rules, rather than make them up myself. When kids have input on rules, they are more likely to buy into them. So, together we'll make up the rules and the consequences for breaking them. The rules might not turn out much differently than last year's, but the kids will feel more a part of the process and likely will take more ownership.

Here are the rules from a recent camp:

COUSIN CAMP RULES

Indoors
When you wake up in the morning, quietly leave the bedroom and come upstairs to the sun porch to see Nana and watch cartoons.
After breakfast, brush your teeth.
Get dressed and make your bed.
Keep your clothes picked up and put away; store shoes under your bed.

Outdoors
You MUST wear your lifejacket whenever you go near the lake, the boats, and the docks.
Hang your beach towel on the clothesline before you come in.
Set lifejackets on the wall outside to dry.
If you ride a bicycle, you MUST wear a helmet.

Toys
SHARE!
Play and put away!
General
Respect each other's property.
Respect each other's privacy.
Treat your cousins like you would treat your friends.

Camp Golden Rule
"Do unto others as you would have them do unto you!"

As you can see from that list, my rules pertain to both safety and respect. They're not outside the bounds of reason; they're just common sense, common courtesy rules. But again, this is not boot camp, and I'm not a drill sergeant. I'm just a grandmother who would like to be able to walk from bed to bed without tripping over sweatshirts and damp bath towels and toys. I let my grandkids be messy within reason—meaning they have their own personal space. If they don't spill into others' territory (which I delineate) and they don't leave wet towels on the carpet, then we're going to be okay.

I have dressers that my grandkids can use, and some use these while others simply live out of their suitcases for the week (or unceremoniously dump the contents of their suitcases into the dresser). Again, that's their choice, so long as their suitcases are not in the way or space of others.

Speaking of towels, my grandkids used to have running battles about who took whose beach towel or bath towel. I finally took care of that by embroidering beach and bath towels with their names on them. Now there's no argument about whose bath towel is left on the floor or about who has whose beach towel.

MORE KIDS, MORE RULES

By the time my grandson Max was ten, he had already been to five Cousin Camps. He had gone from two kids at camp to eight—and suddenly he was aware of all these rules in place. He also wasn't so keen on sharing his Nana and Papa with so many siblings and cousins. "Nana," he said near the beginning of that sixth camp, "I liked Cousin Camp better when there weren't so many rules!"

What he didn't realize is that he *did* have rules when he was five and six (and seven and eight and nine). Those rules in his younger years were in place to protect him and make life pleasant. Now, at age ten, some rules were in place that affected his actions—such as he couldn't be out on the raft between 1 and 2 p.m. because that was the younger girls' time on the raft.

So the rules shift from year to year according to need and situation. Max didn't happen to like the new rule because it infringed on his own freedom. Sometimes the more kids you have, the more rules you need.

How Many Rules?

I don't like to go too rule-crazy. Find the balance that's best for you. Think in terms of what will provide for the grandkids' safety and what will make life more pleasant for everyone.

You have to find that fine line between too many rules and not enough rules. Too many rules drive the kids (and you) crazy and put the focus on following rules, rather than having fun and building relationships. Not enough rules can lead to safety issues, arguments and fights, and bedlam and chaos. Not a pretty picture either way you go.

So how *should* you go?

Draw up rules based on your grandkids' needs. If you have grandchildren who are a little on the "wild side," then create whatever rules you need to create to keep them (and your house) safe. If you have grandkids who are naturally inquisitive (and whose grandkids aren't?), make it clear to them what is off-limits in your house and outside (Grandpa's power tools and your cleansers and knife drawer are good starting points).

I could make a rule that I must be able to bounce a dime off a made bed each morning, but what's the point in that? To be honest, I'm just happy if the beds are still in the same bedrooms when I wake up in the morning (just kidding). If my grandchildren's clothes are in some sort of structured pile, and they can tell what's clean and what's dirty, I'm good with that.

Do I ever have to repeat rules? I *know* you know the answer to that one. Of course I do—especially about clothes and wet towels. (Heck, I'm still reminding Roger about *his* clothes and towels; why should my grandchildren not need a few reminders?) But I don't make a big deal of it. I just remind them, and they pick up their towels or collect their clothing into a little neater pile, and life goes on.

One nice thing about rules: They tend to keep things fair in the kids' minds. They figure if they all live by the same rules, no one gets away with anything, and everyone has the same consequences for breaking the rules.

To be honest, I focus much less on rules than I do on our relationship when our grandkids are with us. I don't want them to sit around thirty years from now and say, "Hey, remember all the cool rules we had at Nana and Papa's house?" "Yeah, weren't they fun?" (Like *that* conversation would ever happen.) Rather, I want them to say, "Didn't we have a great time at Nana and Papa's house?" I want them to treasure our relationships, not our rules.

RULES ARE MADE TO BE BROKEN

Sometimes you have to know when it's okay to break the rules. For example, when Lane was five years old and at her first Cousin Camp, she didn't quite get that she had some chores to do, such as helping to clear the table. After dinner that first evening, I said, "Lane, honey, it's time for you to help clear the table." She squiggled her nose and looked at me like I was speaking Russian. She then looked behind her to see if possibly there was another child named Lane to whom Nana was speaking. Then she shrugged, gave me another strange look, and walked away. I think she actually thought it was a joke.

Morgan, Lane's oldest sister (and always happy to see the "baby" get in trouble), came up to me and said, "What are you going to do, Nana?"

I thought for a moment and said, "Do you think we should enforce the rule?"

She laughed and said, "Nah. I'll help you."

Lane was too young yet for that rule. She had come to Cousin Camp thinking it was all about her. Certainly, she wouldn't have to work at a camp that was all about her!

I chose to be flexible. And the next year, she pitched in with no complaints.

.. .. ..

So there you have it. Routines and rules are great tools to use, but they aren't the be-all and end-all. Use them to get the most out of your time with your grandkids—and keep your time focused on having fun while building relationships.

CHAPTER 3:
Building Relationships

The heart of this book is really about building relationships with your grandchildren. That's what "being intentional" is all about, and that's the primary purpose of my Cousin Camps.

This chapter will give you some ideas about how to build those relationships through a variety of activities that you and your grandkids can do together. I've included ideas for:

- creative and artistic activities
- sports and physical activities
- character-building activities
- faith building activities
- science activities
- adventure activities
- low-cost or no-cost activities

These are "starter" ideas for you, meant to spur your own thinking. As you browse through the activity ideas, consider what types of activities and games would be most appropriate for you and your grandchildren. What would your grandkids enjoy the most? What would stretch their imaginations, help them learn, challenge them, and be barrels of fun? What would make your time together most memorable, and leave them wanting to come back again? (No, I don't mean giving them all the ice cream they can eat!)

Ask yourself these and similar questions as you peruse the ideas in this chapter. Sometimes I'll provide specific examples of activities we do and sometimes I'll just give general suggestions. If you are looking for more ideas in a particular area (say, arts and crafts), visit your library or a local bookstore or look online for ideas. Many entire books are devoted to activities for kids.

This chapter is not meant to be an exhaustive compilation of activities and games you can use. It's meant to give you some ideas and point you in the right direction. Your compass should always be guiding you toward the activities that will be meaningful, fun, and memorable for your grandkids—and will help you deepen your relationship with them.

Creative and Artistic Activities

It's amazing how much fun kids can have with some of the simplest materials—and how they can use those materials to create some of the most treasured pieces of art. You can use finger paints, construction paper, play dough, crayons, pipe cleaners, and a plethora of other materials that are readily available to tap into your grandkids' creativity.

A couple of pointers with these activities: Limit your corrections and expectations of what a finished piece should look like. As I noted earlier, kids see the world through different eyes; take joy in how they do so. Also, if you are crafting along with your grandkids, create something that can't be compared to theirs. For example, if they are painting a nature scene, you could paint a person's face or a house. If you are painting the same thing, they might be discouraged if they see that yours is better.

Here are a couple of ideas to get you thinking.

Princess or Magician Wands

Many young girls love princess wands (and what boy wouldn't want a magician's wand?). Kids can easily make these wands. Here's what you need:

- three-quarter-inch clear vinyl tubing
- corks
- buttons, jewels, glitter, etc.

You can find the tubing at a hardware store. Cut the tubing into 12-inch or 14-inch sections. Place a cork in one end (a wine cork cut in half, to provide both corks, is the perfect size). Partially fill the tube—now a wand—with water. Drop buttons, beads, jewels, glitter, or whatever else into the wand. Add more water until the tube is filled. Cork the other end. Voila! Your grandkids have the perfect, personalized princess or magician's wand. They can decorate the outsides of the wands with markers if they'd like.

Mouse Pads

Older kids who use computers at home might enjoy making mouse pads. Here's what you need:
- foam paper (a heavier type of construction paper)
- liquid squeeze-bottle paint
- transparent contact paper

We use black 8.5 x 11-inch foam paper, but it comes in all colors. The kids create their artwork on it and let it dry. (If you'd like, you can cut the pad to "mouse pad" size before you begin to decorate.) Then they cover it with the contact paper to give it a smooth surface for the mouse.

Stepping Stones

If you have a place in your yard for stepping stones, this activity is a great way to use your grandkids' artwork to beautify your surroundings.

My original idea here was to pour my own stones and let the kids put their hand or foot imprints on them. Eventually, with ten children, my hope was that someday I would have enough stones to do a patio. Someday I might still be able to do that; however, purchasing prepackaged kits is expensive, so I decided to mix and pour my own. Not as easy as you might think! After several debacles, it occurred to me to buy precast stones and acrylic paints and let the kids paint them. I then sprayed them heavily with a sealer to preserve them as long as possible.

So, with that in mind, here's what you need:
- A pre-poured stepping stone for each grandchild
- Acrylic paints

Let the kids paint the stones. Once they dry, place them where you want them.

Stirring the stepping stone mix.

My Creative and Artistic Activities Ideas

List your own ideas for creative activities that you'd like to look into for your grandkids.

_____

_____

_____

_____

_____

_____

Sports and Physical Activities

Most kids love being active. It's likely that they have a number of favorite games that they play with their friends; first tap into their favorites. But sometimes it takes many kids to play a game properly, and if you have just a few grandchildren (or only one), you will need to have some ideas that will work for them.

The PBS website (www.pbskids.org/zoom/activities/games/) has a number of great ideas for physical activities, including sports, relay races, physical challenges, and chase games. There are many other websites and many books that are devoted to physical activities for kids.

One idea is to concoct a "mini-Olympics" of fun and wacky physical activities, all of which could be done in a backyard or a park.

My Sports and Physical Activities Ideas

Note your ideas for physical activities and sports that would suit your grandkids.

_____

_____

_____

_____

_____

_____

Character-Building Activities

Find service-oriented activities in your neighborhood or city. Perhaps you know of an elderly neighbor who needs leaves raked, a homeless shelter that needs help serving meals, or a service organization that needs some helping hands in a project that would be suitable for your grandkids. Churches, communities and local media are also good sources for service-oriented projects that will help build character in your grandchildren and give them a sense of satisfaction for providing help where needed.

Another route to take here is to discuss moral and ethical issues, presenting kids with real-life situations in which choices must be made. For example: On Friday afternoon after school, Zach invites Jason to come over on Saturday morning to play. Jason says yes. But on Saturday morning, Jason wakes up and just feels like watching cartoons and hanging around the house. He asks his mom to call Zach's mom and tell her that he is sick and can't come over.

A few questions to discuss here might include:
- What should Jason's mom do?
- Is it okay to cancel the play date? Why or why not?
- Is it okay to fib about Jason being sick? Why or why not?
- How will Zach feel if he finds out that Jason just didn't want to come over?
- Should Zach's feelings factor into Jason's decision? If so, how?
- What should Jason do?

You can think of these types of moral dilemmas on your own, or find resources at the library or on the Internet to assist you.

My Character-Building Activities Ideas

Jot down some ideas for character-building activities that you'd like to try.

_____

_____

_____

_____

_____

_____

Faith Building Activities

There are a number of sites where you can go online and print coloring pages with Biblical themes. (One such example is www. dltk-bible.com.) Often, kids like to color the same picture that their sibling or cousin is coloring; by printing from websites, you can print as many pages of the same picture as you need. You can also find plenty of Bible activity and coloring books in stores.

You can find oodles of Christian-based puzzles, games, crafts, and activities at www.dltk-bible.com and other websites.

My Faith Building Activities Ideas

Do you have some specific ideas for Faith Building activities you'd like to do with your grandkids? If so, write them here.

_____

_____

_____

_____

_____

_____

Science Activities

Most kids greatly enjoy exploring the world around them. They have a fascination for nature from the teeny-tiny (like examining caterpillars and ladybugs) to the immense (like asking questions about the sun and the moon and the stars). You can find great books and videos and other resources that help them learn about whatever they're interested in—and you can also find resources to help you conduct fun experiments and activities that both entertain and lead to new knowledge. Just Google "science experiments for kids" and you'll find a great number (over one million) websites with experiments and activities.

My Science Activities Ideas

What types of science activities would you like to try with your grandkids?

_____

_____

_____

_____

_____

_____

Adventure Activities

"Adventure activities" can be as far-ranging as cool interactive adventure games on the Internet (www.nationalgeographic.com/kids/games has a number of them, for one example) to adventures that take place in a nearby park, a forest preserve, or your own back yard. You are limited only by your own (and your grandkids') imaginations here. A couple of examples of adventure activities include theme-based adventures (pirates or princesses or explorers or anything else) and treasure hunts with the kids searching for a series of clues that lead to their treasure.

Another way to think of adventure is to take the mundane—for example, breakfast—and make it _not_ so mundane. For example, on occasion we'll have a simple campfire breakfast, cooking sausage, eggs, hash browns, and biscuits. It's outdoors, the kids love the idea of a campfire in the morning, and it's a great—and different—way to start our day. Adventures don't need to be elaborate; they just need to be interesting and fun and "out of the ordinary"!

My Adventure Activities Ideas

List ideas you have for adventure activities.

_____

_____

_____

_____

_____

_____

Low-Cost or No-Cost Activities

Quite often the activities that kids love most happen to be low-cost or no-cost activities. If you Google "low-cost activities for kids," you will find thousands of sites brimming with ideas for activities you can do for free or for a minimal amount of money.

A handful of ideas include:

- Put on a theatrical performance.
- Build a fun house.
- Make a trivia game of words and definitions to play another day.
- Draw a self-portrait to frame and put up on your wall.
- Create a food sculpture and then eat it.
- Have a talent show.
- Make friendship jewelry.
- Have a puppet show.

One activity I have my grandkids do is create a time capsule. They fill out a sheet that asks them about their favorite (and least favorite) things to do, their favorite books and songs, their favorite TV show, their best friend, and so on. They also have to write what they think they will be like in five years and in ten years. I then keep these "capsules" and will share them with them in five and ten years. It's fun for them and for me, too, as I witness their growth and share in their hopes and dreams. See Appendix D for a sample time capsule.

I've also saved all my Christmas cards for a few years, cut out the pictures, and had my grandkids use the pictures to create collages or to turn non-Christmassy cards into birthday cards. The cards also come in handy as models for the kids when they are drawing—for example, they pull out a picture of a bear to help them as they draw their own bear.

Another low-cost activity we do—and one that focuses on building relationships today while carrying on family tradition and heritage—is having a tea party for the girls. We use their great grandmother's antique tea service, with silver pot and flowered teacups, and I buy large, inexpensive, different-colored sun hats for the girls to wear. They decorate their hats with ribbons and silk flowers from my closet, and help set the table with teacups and nameplates for each setting. We put out finger sandwiches and cookies to nibble on while we have our tea—which, by the way, is raspberry ice tea, because it's too hot to drink hot tea in the summer. We pour the ice tea out of the pot and have a grand old time while Papa takes the boys fishing (for which they get up at the crack of dawn) and later to Dairy Queen and miniature golfing. So both the boys and the girls get their special day.

Here's another idea: Save egg cartons, toilet paper rolls, yogurt cups, and so on, in boxes or plastic containers and stuff them in the back of a closet, and pull them out when the grandkids come. They can decorate the items with colors, paint, colored paper, or whatever art material you have. Just let them use their imaginations. (This is an especially good idea for any unexpected visits.)

It's amazing what uses (artsy-craftsy and otherwise) kids can find for the most mundane items: paper towel tubes, yogurt cups, shoe boxes, and so on. I keep a closet filled with what most people would consider trash—but my grandkids see it as a storehouse for fun.

Nothing like a stylish tea party to brighten the day.

My Low-Cost or No-Cost Activities Ideas

Note ideas you have for low-cost or no-cost activities.

_____

_____

_____

_____

_____

_____

Involve Your Grandchildren

If you're searching for ideas, sometimes the best place to go is to the activity centers themselves: your grandkids. Count on them to come up with some good ideas (after all, who knows what's fun better than they do?).

You can involve them in another way, too, in the "pre-activity" phase. If you're doing a craft that calls for a collection of pinecones or acorns, have them go outside (under your supervision) to do the collecting. This saves you time and makes them feel that they've contributed. They're bound to like the project better, because they were in on the "ground floor."

Do the Unexpected

Kids *love* zany ideas—anything that is unusual, unexpected, or that turns things upside down and makes them look at the world in a whole new way.

Like Christmas in July, mentioned earlier, we decorated a Christmas tree, exchanged gifts, sang carols, the whole works! They loved it, as did I.

Are you getting together with your grandkids in winter? Then how about a Hawaiian surfing theme? Or why reserve Thanksgiving for one day a year? Have Thanksgiving in the spring! Mix it up, and have fun.

And, Speaking of the Unexpected ...

You're tired. You've been running low on energy all day. The doorbell rings. You open the door to see your daughter with her three young kids, who are all smiling up at you. Your daughter asks you, rather sheepishly, if you could "at the last minute" watch the kids for a while; her sitter fell through and she's got a meeting she can't miss.

Naturally, you smile and say, "Of course! What a delight!"

And as the kids scramble past you, you wonder, "What should we do?" (Or perhaps it's more like, "What should we do that won't drain me of what little energy I have at the moment?")

I'd like to make three points about these types of encounters:

1. Keep a list of activity ideas handy.

Keep a list or folder of ideas that you can pull out for those unexpected occasions (or what I refer to as "drive-by drop-offs"). As you create lists or make plans for some of the activity areas mentioned earlier in this chapter, collect those ideas in a binder or folder. For example, maybe you can take a trip to see a new museum or new park.

Planning is the key here. Always be looking for ideas and jot them down when you find them, to help you with those spur-of-the-moment visits. Then you won't be so frantic when your son or daughter shows up on your doorstep unexpectedly, with kids in tow.

2. Make the encounter meaningful—no matter how tired you are, no matter how unprepared you are for it.

Maybe you were caught off guard. Maybe you had plans for a brief nap, followed by a few errands or some shopping.

But don't let the grandkids see that. Let them see the pleasure and excitement in your eyes. Be a "cup half full" person. Don't see the lost opportunity for napping or shopping; see the gained opportunity to spend time with your grandkids.

Want to start out on the right foot? Then get down on eye level with your grandkids. Smile, give them your undivided attention, and hug and lovingly touch them.

3. Be intentional—even about these unexpected encounters.

This really ties in with my first point about being prepared for unexpected visits. Be ready to make every visit— planned and unplanned—a positive, fun, uplifting time for you and your grandkids. When you're intentional, you can shift gears even if you're not ready for a visit and make it a meaningful time.

Keys to Building Strong Relationships with Your Grandkids

Let's be honest: Some personalities grate on you, while others are easy to get along with. When someone is easier to get along with or has a personality that we really appreciate, it's easy to gravitate toward that person and be more attentive to that person.

Let's say you have two grandkids, Jimmy and Shannon. Jimmy is an easy-going, pleasant boy who is polite, respectful, and generally cheerful. Shannon is fiery, strong-willed, temperamental, critical, and tends to see the glass as half empty. Sometimes she can make life miserable.

It would be very easy to want to spend more time with Jimmy. But if you do, Shannon will pick up on this, and it will drive a rift between you and her. If you want to build a strong relationship with Shannon, you need to spend the time and attention it takes to do that.

Choose to overlook the challenging parts of her personality and figure out how to love her. In turn, she'll love you. Don't take her personality as an affront—it's not. Try to understand where she's coming from and what makes her tick.

I have a grandchild who is a born worrier—she even asks me if I have enough gas in the car. I could react by being offended or annoyed, but then I realize how awful it must be to worry about things like that at her age. I immediately feel compassion and reassure her that she will be taken care of and everything is fine.

The point is this: Don't do what's easiest for you. Do what's best for the child.

The nice thing is, in the long run, it's also best for you.

Following are some of the keys to building a strong relationship with your grandchildren.

Feelings often follow actions. Hug that "unhuggable" child. Smile at that moody, temperamental child. You might be surprised at what follows.

Love and Acceptance

Every good relationship is built on love. See the uniqueness in each grandchild; appreciate the God-given gifts and abilities and personality of each child. Let them know, through your actions, that they are loved for who they are—imperfections and all.

Focus on who they are and what their unique strengths and traits are, rather than trying to change them into who you want them to be. Accept them unconditionally, be supportive, and gently guide them as the opportunities arise.

That doesn't mean you turn a blind eye to misbehavior, be it from a four-year-old or an eighteen-year-old. When they've done something wrong, large or small, confront them with it, but wrap that confrontation in love. Tell them you love them and they can't do anything that can make you stop loving them. You might not love what they're doing or what they just did, but you love *them* and that won't stop.

Empathy and Understanding

Empathy ranges from cleaning and bandaging skinned knees (and drying tear-streaked cheeks) of a five-year-old to consoling an eleven-year-old after a tough basketball game to listening to the dating or friendship woes of a sixteen-year-old—with many pit stops in between.

Give your grandkids a safe place to talk, no matter the situation or issue. Show them by your interactions with them that you are aware of and sensitive to their feelings, thoughts, and experiences. This goes a long way to building a trusting relationship with them.

Again, this doesn't mean you have to condone poor judgment or behavior on their part. It means you are empathetic to what they are experiencing or feel, regardless of how those experiences or feelings originated.

Time

Time—that is, your giving of it—is one of the primary ways to show your love for your grandkids. If you're not retired, time can be harder to come by. Even if you are retired, time is not always easy to come by.

Time is free, yet it's priceless. Once we've lost it, we can't get it back. If we don't make time for our grandkids, we lose out. And we lose *them*.

Communication

Communication is, of course, a key to any relationship. Do whatever you have to do to keep the lines of communication open between you and your grandkids. A few pointers:

- Pay attention to them and show your interest in what they are saying. If you give them an absent-minded "Mm-hmm" while you are folding laundry as they are telling you something near and dear to their heart, the next time they have something important to say, they might choose to say it to someone else.
- Respect what they say. Hide your initial reactions, no matter how outlandish or crazy their ideas might seem. If you look shocked or annoyed or amused, they might shut down.
- Don't be quick to judge, and don't play favorites. If Michael and Jenna each blame the other for starting a fight, don't assume that the more congenial and gentle child is the one in the right.
- Don't try to talk their talk. Talk like a fifty-, sixty-, or seventy-year-old, not a fifteen-year-old. Don't try to adopt their lingo; you'll just sound foolish and phony. It's appropriate—even necessary—to understand their lingo, but keep to what's natural for you when talking with them. If you start trying to talk like a fifteen-year-old (and believe me, you'll fail), they'll start wondering who you are.
- Give them a safe place to talk. When kids feel safe, welcome, and appreciated, they'll talk. When your relationship is genuine and built on mutual trust and love, they'll talk. If, on the other hand, they think that you're just ferreting out information to pass along to their parents or that you're going to pass judgment on them, they'll clam up. Once that happens, it's hard to get them to open up again.

Accountability

Safety, empathy, and love—all points brought up earlier in talking about the keys to a good relationship with your grandkids—don't negate the need for accountability. Kids need to be held accountable for their actions; they need to know that their behavior has consequences. Good behavior has good consequences (an ice cream outing, play time in the park); misbehavior has its consequences as well (sitting on the sidelines while others play, not going to a movie as planned).

You are doing your grandkids a favor when you hold them accountable. You are teaching them a lesson that has value throughout their lifetimes. Most kids respect the need for borders and limits to their actions, and to being held accountable for what they say and do. They not only need it; they expect it. It makes them feel safe, secure, and loved.

Being in Accord with Parents

Yes, things can be different at your house. You can have your own "Nana Rules," which might include ice cream for breakfast (at least the kids will get their milk), or staying up a half hour later to play games or finish a movie. But you need to be in accord with the important rules and values that are in place at your grandkids' houses. Primarily we're talking behavior and language here. Don't let them watch movies or use language that their parents don't approve; don't allow them to fight or argue or behave in ways that would get them in trouble at home.

In other words, a visit to the grandparents doesn't give grandkids a free pass to act however they want and say whatever they please.

That being said, let your grandkids know that while you respect the rules in their house, it's okay to have a few special rules (like that ice cream for breakfast) at your house. Just don't go against any important rule that their parents have established. When you have that ice cream for breakfast, let them know that you agree with their parents' rule that ice cream is normally not for breakfast, but that at Nana's house you can bend that rule once in a while. Keep the respect for the parents, and make it clear that this is a momentary bending of the rule in your house, not a refuting of it.

If you don't make it clear that you're just momentarily bending a rule, you could have an issue on your hands. That's what the next chapter is about: handling issues.

CHAPTER 4:

In the best of relationships, in the cheeriest of homes, in the most serene of times, there are issues. They can range from small ("Who left their wet bath towel on the floor?") to large ("Who backed out of the garage—while the garage door was still down?") to everything in between.

Many say that grandparenting is wonderful because we get to enjoy the grandkids without dealing with any of the problems. (Or, as my husband says, "If we'd known how great grandkids are we'd have started with them.") Some grandparents, perhaps subconsciously (or not), take the attitude, "Let's enjoy the grandkids, but when they soil their diapers, start fighting with each other, or bring up their school problems or peer pressure challenges, we'll hand them back to their parents."

Well, that's not the way it works at Cousin Camp. When you spend a week with your grandkids, you can't ignore the problems that arise. I think it's best that you handle them even if you are just spending the afternoon with your grandkids.

Why? Because the better equipped you are to deal with issues, the better things will be for both you and your grandkids. It's like the Boy Scout motto says: Be Prepared. As intentional grandparents, we have to be prepared for anything and everything.

Here are a few of the issues that you might face, and some suggestions for handling them.

Homesickness

This typically won't apply if your grandkids aren't spending multiple overnights with you. But if they're spending a week with you, or even several days, you might see signs of homesickness: sadness, tears, not wanting to do much, and not eating well, to mention a few. Many kids will be forthright about their feelings, saying they miss their parents or they want to talk to them or go home.

Younger kids especially can be prone to separation anxiety. In my Cousin Camp, the kids must be five years old before they first attend, partly for this very reason.

So what can you do about homesick kids? The best defense against homesickness is:

- Acknowledge their homesickness,
- Make them feel loved and important,
- Keep them distracted and busy, and
- Fill their day with fun activities.

It's important to acknowledge their homesickness because in doing so, you are showing the empathy that's so crucial to building the good relationships that we talked about in the previous chapter. Of course, each child responds differently to empathy; some will get sadder if you focus too much on their woes. Don't dwell on their sadness, but do acknowledge it by saying something like, "I know you miss your mom and dad, and that's perfectly natural. We'll give them a call a little later on. But if you could help me gather some kindling and wood for our campfire, then soon we'll be roasting marshmallows for our s'mores. You do like s'mores, don't you?" (I've never received a "No" to that question.)

Distract them with something immediate—in this case, getting a campfire going, with the intent of making s'mores—and make them feel loved and important. Kids love helping out, whether it's collecting kindling and wood for a campfire, collecting leaves or acorns for an art project, or washing Grandpa's car; it makes them feel needed and useful. Feeling that way makes them feel important—which, of course, they are. Look for tangible ways to help them feel that way.

You can also distract them with things that will take place the next day. Especially in the evening, kids like to look forward to what's going to happen tomorrow. If they're feeling a bit blue in the evening, talk about the fun events you have planned for tomorrow. Get their minds focused on all the fun they're going to have.

When kids are having fun, it's pretty much impossible to be homesick. Just as "perfect love casts out fear" (1 John 4:18), so "great fun casts out homesickness." The two can't coexist. This isn't the only reason that you want to plan to have lots of fun with your grandkids, but it's certainly effective for those homesick youngsters who are all teary-eyed and thinking about how much they miss Mom and Dad.

TOUGH TIME FOR FIRST-TIMER

When my granddaughter Morgan was five, she was a first-time camper joining her brother and cousin—both of whom had been there the previous year and had really bonded. Morgan was very close to her brother, but he was off having fun with his cousin, leaving her alone and moping and missing home.

I remember seeing Morgan one early evening at a weenie roast we were having down by the lake. She was perched on the bank, circling a stick in the water, resting her chin on her hand and looking glum. My heart just bled for her. I sat beside her, hugged her, and gave her a kiss.

"I miss my Mom," she said, and a tear trickled down her cheek.

"I know you do, sweetie." I hugged her again and comforted her. As she snuggled against me, sniffling a little, I said, "Would you do me a favor? Would you roast my hot dog for me? I never seem to get mine just right."

She sniffed a bit more and nodded; this perked her up a bit. As she roasted the hot dog, I talked about what we were going to do that next day—which included miniature golfing, something she loves. Later, I discreetly reminded her brother and cousin to include Morgan in their activities, to "take her under their wing," so to speak. They stepped up to the task, feeling important about showing a first-time camper the ropes, and by the next day all was well.

Sometimes intentional grandparenting includes
soothing homesick hearts.

Sibling or Cousin Rivalries

Yes, brothers and sisters and cousins can often have great fun together. Unfortunately, they can also have rivalries that pop up and cause problems. Sometimes the rivalries are front and center, and sometimes they're disguised and subtle. Sometimes you know about them in advance, and sometimes they appear for the first time.

So what do you do when you notice a rivalry emerging? First, you acknowledge it. Then you do whatever you need to do to effectively snuff it out.

Quite often these tiffs come about when one person is upset with another and immediately starts pointing out all the faults of the other. Sometimes it's about size (particularly if a child is large or small); other times it centers on a person's looks or habits or traits. If you have a grandchild who is being teased for being big for their age, it's no use denying it. Use the opportunity to say, "We're all different in lots of ways. That doesn't make any one of us right and the others wrong. God made us all different, and He gave us specific qualities and abilities, and it's good how He made us." It's important to recognize that differences are okay, and that we should look for the positives in our differences—such as, "He's going to be a great football player some day." Or, point out that girls tend to grow faster and a girl who is bigger today might not be bigger in a few years.

Does that mean that saying something along those lines will curb all rivalries? No. But it will let the kids know what you think about them picking on each other and that you won't tolerate that behavior. It does tend to lessen the intensity of the rivalry, in my experience.

Note that you don't have to step in to "officiate" whenever you see or hear something that signals a rivalry issue is heating up. Many comments or actions that might be coming from rivalries are quickly snuffed out on their own. Gauge your stepping in by how the kids involved are faring. If one is being hurt (physically or emotionally), then step in. If no one seems to be bothered by it, then there's no reason for you to be, either.

Sometimes all the kids need is "the look" from Grandma. "The look" needs no verbal interpretation—they know what it means!

Other Behavior Issues

For most behavior issues, I take the Barney Fife stance: I "nip it in the bud." Barney, the deputy sheriff on *The Andy Griffith Show*, was famous for nipping lots of buds. I'd say (thankfully) that that's perhaps the only similarity Barney and I share, but nipping is the best way to deal with undesirable behavior.

Essentially, that means if kids are fighting or arguing, I separate them immediately. When they can behave properly, I let them back in the game or whatever it is we're doing.

I don't believe in the traditional timeout, where the offending party is sent to his or her room. This isn't really a punishment as much as it is a break for the child, who oftentimes wants to get away from the current scene, anyway. The bigger punishment is to have the child remain in the same setting but not take part in the activity until he or she can regain self-control (and, as the case warrants it, can sincerely apologize). If you're playing softball or wiffle ball, and Nathan is misbehaving, have Nathan sit on the sidelines until he's ready to be civil and rejoin the action. If Nathan has been fighting with Sarah, bring the two back together after Nathan has calmed down and have Nathan apologize. If he does so sincerely, then he's back in the game.

I view a timeout as a copout. Kids don't deal with issues in a timeout. Help them work through the issues.

I have friends who handle arguments between their kids this way: Rather than listen to heated explanations of "he said/she said," they send the kids to a central location in their house, within sight of the parents. The kids sit there until they can agree on what happened; then they return to the parents. They agree on who will tell their story, and that child tells his version of what happened. A parent asks the other child if this is accurate; if he says "No," then they return to the steps and repeat the process until they can mutually agree on what happened. If they can't agree on the story after three tries, they both lose privileges; if they do agree on what happened within three tries, the offender loses privileges , but to a lesser degree than if they hadn't come to an agreement on what happened.

My friends assure me that this works, so I'm going to try it for my next Cousin Camp.

Obedience issues aren't a problem for us. Our grandkids have been raised to respect their elders and to do as they're told. Even so, this year I'm going to clearly spell out behavior rules and the consequences for breaking those rules. The kids will have a say in the rules and the consequences. Once they're decided, we'll post the rules and the consequences on the family room wall. Giving the kids a say in the rules and the consequences gives them some ownership and helps them to buy into the plan. It's just one more way to help things run smoothly at camp.

Just broken up a heated argument? Give it a little time before you address the issue. When your own emotions—and those of your grandkids—calm down, you can address the issue more rationally.

"WHO'S THE BOSS?"

The four sons of friends of mine used to constantly fight about who gets to sit in the front seat, who gets to pick out the family movie to watch, and so on. So the parents devised a weekly calendar with a "Leader of the Day" (along with all the daily activities) noted for each day. The leader receives first choice in any matter about which the brothers bicker: where to sit at the table, where to go for ice cream, what type of pizza to get, etc. The next day's leader gets second choice. It works, because each boy knows his day will come.

I used a version of this last year when I had nine grandkids at my camp. I paired kids up in teams of two to take care of chores such as cleaning the table or taking out the trash. The ninth child became my Special Agent in Charge (SAC). That person had a black cap with "SAC" on it, and the SAC got to do the special things with me: walk to the mailbox a hundred yards or so down the road, feed and walk the dog, and so on. Virtually anything the SAC got to do—including mundane things like taking recyclables to the garage—became special simply because they were the only kid who got to do it. Just as my friends changed their leader every day, I changed my SAC each day.

Parental Issues

Issues with the parents of your grandkids will likely be at a minimum because, let's face it, parents are typically happy to get a break, and most parents want their kids to develop stronger relationships with grandparents. So they're happy their kids are going to spend time with Grandma and Grandpa, no questions asked.

Still, I think it's not only helpful, but important, to clearly communicate both orally (in person or over the phone) and in writing exactly what you plan for the time the grandkids will be with you. See the letter in Chapter 1 for a sample of how I communicate with parents prior to the camp.

An issue that might arise is one of a parent intruding too much—particularly one who calls a homesick child too often. I find it helpful to set times when we will call the parents; otherwise, either the child or a parent will call too often, with the result being the child becomes more homesick, not less.

Assure the parents what they already know: that you love their children, that their children's safety and well-being is of utmost importance to you, and that you will take great care of them and have a fun time planned.

Sometimes parents have a bit of separation anxiety, just as kids do, if it's the first time they've been apart from their kids for an extended time. However, once they see their kids return, full of smiles and stories about their time with Grandma and Grandpa, they'll relax and see it for what it is—a blessing for everyone involved.

Illnesses and Injuries

I've been fortunate: In all the years I've been doing Cousin Camp, we haven't had a big illness issue, such as flu being passed around. We've had our share of scraped knees and skinned elbows and of bumps and bruises from falling off of bikes or out of trees, but we haven't had anything too major. Nothing that a few ice packs, a couple of Tylenol, a little soap, and a few Band-Aids couldn't handle (along with a little T.L.C. delivered by Nana).

According to Mayo Clinic, the top five illnesses that kids get (and the ways to treat them) are:
1. *Colds*. Treat with pain relievers, decongestant nasal sprays, and cough syrups.
2. *Stomach flu (gastroenteritis)*. Suck on ice chips; keep hydrated. Also drink water, 7-Up or Sprite, Gatorade,

and clear broths. Ease back into eating with crackers and toast. Get plenty of rest.

3. *Ear infections.* See a doctor.
4. *Pink eye (conjunctivitis).* See a doctor.
5. *Sore throats.* Get rest and keep hydrated with water, soups, and broths. If it doesn't go away in thirty-six hours, see a doctor.

Medical Emergencies

You want to also be prepared for any medical emergencies. If your granddaughter has asthma, make sure she has her inhaler and any other medications that she uses. If your grandson is diabetic, make sure he has his blood sugar monitoring device and medicine with him. In other words, know your grandchildren's medical needs based on their history and know how to respond to those needs (e.g., making sure they are staying on top of their monitoring and medicine schedules). If your grandchild has a disease, you need to know the signs of distress to look for—for example, in type 2 diabetes, frequent urination and extreme thirst are signs the blood sugar is out of whack. You need to know how to respond.

Beyond that, you need to be ready to respond to any other type of medical emergency—anything that would require a trip to the hospital. I have my grandkids' parents sign a medical release (see Appendix E), which I include with the letter that I send to the parents prior to Cousin Camp. This release identifies who I am and gives me permission to take the kids to a medical center for treatment. It also includes a copy of the parents' insurance card.

Medical emergencies are, thankfully, rare, but you want to think them through beforehand and be prepared to act. It makes it much easier to respond in the event of a real emergency.

A Word to the Wise

If you're out on a lake with a child and that child falls in the water, should you (a) jump in and try to help her swim, or (b) stay in the boat and throw her a life preserver?

If you chose "b," you're correct! I say this out of the experience I gained with my daughter when she was in college, but I think that principle translates to younger ages as well. My daughter, years back, was going though sorority recruitment, commonly known as "rush week." She called in tears one day to tell me she thought she had been passed over by her first three choices. I couldn't do anything about it except stew and fret. I tossed and turned in bed that night, hearing my daughter's broken voice over and over again.

So, the next day, I called her to see if she was okay. I was ready to console her as best I could.

She was not just okay; she was fine. It turned out she got her first choice and had simply forgotten to call me. I was happy for her, yes, but also a little perturbed that she hadn't called to let me know. (After all, she thought to call me about the *bad* news!)

I learned from that experience that I should have just stayed in the boat and not, emotionally at least, jumped in the water with her. My getting all emotionally wrought up about it did neither her nor me any good.

Kids are tougher and more resilient than we think they are. Remember this when you are handling whatever issues come your way. Stay steady and calm. If they are flailing in the water, throw them a life preserver. But don't jump in after them. You'll just get all wet—and frustrated.

Hopefully this chapter answered many questions you might have had about handling issues. But I know you likely still have more questions—and I will address those in the next chapter.

CHAPTER 5:
Yes, You Can Do This

Almost everyone I talk to likes the idea of Cousin Camp. They can readily see the benefits that I mentioned in the Introduction. Who wouldn't want to:

- spend more time with their grandchildren,
- develop deeper relationships with them,
- help cousins to get to know each other better,
- pass down family traditions, and
- simply enjoy their grandchildren while they can?

When we become intentional about our grandparenting, we can do all this and more. No doubt you can add other benefits to that list, benefits that are specific to your own relationships with your grandchildren.

So we know the upside, and because the upside is strong, we know it is well worth the effort.

But some of you might be concerned about what you see as the downside: your ability to set up your own camp. You're not sure you're up to the task. Sure, I've done it, you might say. So it's easy for me to say that it's not hard to pull off. But let me assure you, I entered my first camp with more trepidation than confidence and more questions than answers.

Going into your first camp, it's natural that you are going to have more questions than answers. No matter how much you read about it and think about it, you haven't done it. You have to experience it for yourself and know that it's okay to have some doubts entering in.

That said, I'm going to do my best to dispel as many of those doubts as possible. I've already gone over many of the issues that you might face and how to handle them, in the previous chapter. Here I'm going to focus on concerns that you and your children and children-in-law might have about the camp.

Concerns Grandparents Might Have

I have addressed some of the questions in this section in earlier chapters, but I want to touch on them again because they are some of the primary concerns that grandparents have. Other questions in here bring up new subjects.

Q: I'm not sure if I'm close enough to my grandkids. They probably won't want to do this.

A: One of the primary reasons you're doing this is to become closer to your grandkids. So don't worry about how close you are *now*; focus on how your camp will help you get closer to them.

Remember, all kids love attention. A lot of times, with today's ultra-fast pace and maxed-out schedules, that one-on-one attention with parents dwindles to almost nothing. So if your grandkids know you are planning time for them and want them to come over, be it for an afternoon or an overnighter or a week, chances are they'll appreciate it (and you).

Sure, some kids might come in doubting that they will have a lot of fun. So it's up to you to surprise them with fun activities that they'll want to do. The activity ideas in Chapter 3 should give you a good start on planning the fun time that will help you and your grandkids draw closer.

Take the initiative. Don't sit back and wait for your grandkids to ask for a camp. If it's what you want, make it happen. Be intentional!

Q: I don't know if I can handle my grandkids. My health isn't the greatest.

A: In Chapter 1, I mentioned that you need to plan according to your health and what you can reasonably handle. If what you can reasonably handle hampers your plans for what you'd like to do (or if you have many grandkids), get help! I enlist the help of a few teenage girls each summer.

Q: I'm not sure what to do with my grandkids. They might get bored.

A: I can all but guarantee you they will get bored—if you don't have a plan. But you will have a plan. Based on what your grandkids like, you'll find appropriate activities, some very physical to burn off their excess energy and some that are sedentary and more calming, such as art projects and indoor games. Give Chapter 3 another look; it has plenty of ideas and leads to great activities. Then plan away!

Q: My grandkids don't get along very well.

A: Sometimes kids don't get along well because there are little (or not so little) rivalries between siblings or cousins. I talked about this in the previous chapter. Reread that portion to get some tips on how to handle such rivalries.

At other times kids don't get along well simply because they aren't normally together, such as the case with cousins who live far apart. It's not that they don't like each other; they simply don't know each other that well—which is one of the primary reasons you're hosting your camp.

I have two thoughts here. First, make the time together so fun—and different from the norm for them—that they don't have time, or the inclination, to not get along or to feel uncomfortable with each other. It's amazing what a different set of circumstances and a little fun can do to change dispositions and rivalries.

Second, and I say this only somewhat with tongue in cheek, if kids aren't getting along well, there's nothing to unite them like giving them a common adversary—meaning you! That is, get their focus off themselves and put it on you. I've noticed when a few grandkids are grumbling or not getting along very well and

I lay down the law, it not only puts their attention on me but gives them a common opponent, if you will (and I do use the terms "adversary" and "opponent" lightly; I don't mean to truly become their enemy).

Or better yet, get their focus on a project with a common goal that helps them pull together and work as a team.

The bottom line is kids often are not going to get along perfectly. Know that going in and you're ahead of the game. Just because your grandkids don't always get along doesn't mean you can't or shouldn't host a camp for them. In fact, look at it the other way: Your camp might be the place where they actually learn to get along a little better.

Q: There's a big age gap among my grandkids.

A: My nine grandkids range in age from six to twelve. Your age range might be even greater than that. What I suggest is this: Split your kids into age-appropriate groups. That is, split them into groups where their interests and abilities and maturity levels are roughly equal.

For me, that means splitting into two groups (six- to eight-year-olds in one group, and ten- to twelve-year-olds in the other). Sometimes we come together for certain activities, and sometimes in those activities I pair older kids with younger ones. I find the older kids like that responsibility of helping the younger kids.

But more often than not, I keep the two groups separate and they do their own age-appropriate activities. These activities are often similar, but I adjust them to be appropriately challenging and fun for each group.

Depending on the number of kids you have and the type of activities you have planned, you might need help.

I knew I needed to split the kids into groups when all nine kids would go play on a huge rubber trampoline that we have moored in the lake near our house. The kids love to bounce on the tramp and jump or dive into the lake off of it. Sometimes a little good-natured roughhousing takes place on it, and kids shove each other off the raft, whooping and hollering and having a blast. Well, the little girls loved jumping off the tramp as much as the older kids, but they didn't like getting shoved off it, especially by older siblings.

So I split the tramp times, giving both older kids and younger kids their own time.

Q: I have too many grandkids to do this!

A: Can we ever have too many grandkids? Remember, you're just doing this for a short time; there is a light at the end of the tunnel (and no, it's not a train headlight). I repeat: Don't overestimate what you can do and don't underestimate what a helper or two can do for you. Just as you might need to split into groups when you have large differences in the ages of your grandkids, you also might need to split into groups if you have a large number of grandkids. When you have the right amount of help, everything goes smoother and everybody—kids and grandparents alike—are happier.

Here's another option to consider, one that I'm considering myself for next year: Splitting the kids into age groups and having only one group at a time at the camp (so, running two camps next year). I know logistically this might not work for everyone, but it's something to consider.

Q: My grandkids aren't the best-behaved kids. I'm concerned about behavior issues that might crop up.

A: Remember, you're the adult. You set the rules and a positive tone. I talked about dealing with behavior issues in the previous chapter; revisit that material. But it boils down to this: Deal with the issues and use common sense.

Maybe it helps that my husband is a big bear of a man with a white beard and a gruff demeanor. When a child or two is having an issue, Roger will butt in and say to the child, "I'm older, bigger, and tougher than you and I'm the boss. So knock it off." And you know what? They knock it off. Even though they know their Papa is a big teddy bear inside, that big gruff demeanor gets them every time. He doesn't even have to say it gruffly; he just naturally growls when he speaks.

You might not have a Roger in your house, but you are the authority. So stand up and use that authority. Stick by the rules you set, or they'll think that they can do anything they want because you won't enforce the rules. Enforce them fairly and not out of anger, but enforce them.

Concerns Grandparents' Children Might Have

Sometimes the grandparents are sold on the idea of Cousin Camp, but it's an idea they have to sell to their children—particularly if the camp is a multi-day one. Here are some of the concerns that your own kids might raise, and ways to answer those concerns.

Q: What if the kids get homesick?
A: Then I will comfort and distract them. I won't pretend they're not homesick; rather, I'll let them know I know they're feeling blue, and I'll make them feel loved and important. I'll set up times when they can call you, but I won't let them (or you) call just whenever, because that tends to feed homesickness. But don't worry; I'll keep them busy and distracted doing fun things, and pretty soon they'll forget that they were homesick!

Q: What if the kids are too much for you?
A: If I thought the kids were going to be too much for me, I wouldn't have planned this time together. I'm ready for this; I have a detailed plan in place. We're going to keep active and busy with lots of fun things. I have two teenage girls—very responsible young ladies—who are going to help me out in the afternoon. It will be fine, because the kids are not running the show. I am. I'm ready for them!

Q: What if there's a medical emergency?
A: Then I will use the medical release form that you signed for me and take them to the hospital. For lesser "emergencies"— cut knees and twisted ankles and such—I am well prepared. Remember, I was a mom before I became a grandma; I've been through a medical emergency or two.

Q: What if I'm just generally uneasy about this and not sure it's the best thing for you?
A: I'm looking forward to a great time with the kids and excited about them coming here. So just kick back, relax, and enjoy the break I'm offering you! After all, if you can't trust your own mother, who can you trust? I know how to care for children (remember?). So give me the benefit of the doubt, and let's give this a try.

CHAPTER 6:
A Win-Win Situation

Okay. I've just spent five chapters explaining the ins and outs of planning and running a Cousin Camp, or whatever you want to call your get-togethers with your grandkids.

I've hammered home the importance of being intentional about spending time with your grandkids and of being intentional regarding how you spend that time.

I've shared various experiences from past Cousin Camps that have both blessed me and instructed me in shaping future camps. Those experiences assured me that though not everything always went smoothly for me, the camps have been, in the end, worth it.

That, of course, has been my motivation for writing this book: My experiences with Cousin Camp have been so rewarding that I felt led to share the idea of such a camp with others, so others could be similarly blessed.

When you try your own version of Cousin Camp, know that not everything will go smoothly. Activities that you were sure would be big hits will fizzle. Laughter and merriment will likely mix with a few tiffs and tears. That beautiful day at the park might be rained out. Your kitchen table might be marked, a glass (or a window) might be broken, or your garage door might be dented.

In other words, Cousin Camp is a lot like life itself—it rarely goes precisely as planned, and always includes a few things you wish didn't happen. Know that going in, be flexible, and keep the big picture in mind.

That's the picture of you and your grandkids smiling cheek to cheek, inseparably bonded. You'll frame it and place it somewhere prominent in your home. More importantly, you'll keep it in your heart forever.

That's what happens when you're intentional about your relationships with your grandkids. When you are intentional, the blessings and benefits far outweigh the perils and pains that present themselves in any relationship when you press on beyond the surface.

Those blessings will fall on both you and your grandkids.

Blessings

Many of the blessings you will experience will be unique to your own relationship with your grandkids. Among those unique blessings, you most likely will experience these:

You and your grandkids will draw closer and develop deeper and more meaningful relationships.

You will create lasting memories for you and for them.

You will pass on traditions and heritage that are unique to your family.

You will create a positive impression on your grandkids and have a positive effect on their lives.

Doubtless you can add to that list. Once you try your own Cousin Camp, I'm sure you will.

The greatest blessings we receive as grandparents are watching grandkids grow up into young men and women—and being an active, integral part of that growing process. That doesn't mean we force ourselves into their lives; it means, by the very relationships we have with them, they *want* us to be an important part of their lives.

I know my grandkids love Cousin Camp because their moms tell me they mention it throughout the year. For example, one older sibling told a younger sibling, after the younger one had gotten in trouble, that she wouldn't be able to attend Cousin Camp that summer. That pronouncement (which wasn't true) produced more tears and fear than the punishment for her minor misbehavior. The older child, in the ancient ways of older children, was simply trying to torture the younger child.

Not long ago I received a drawing in the mail from one of my daughters. Her daughter, in Sunday School, had drawn a picture that represented the idea of "patience." Her drawing was of her waiting patiently for the next Cousin Camp.

Roger and I have received compliments about our grandkids' behavior when we've been with them in restaurants, and last year a flight attendant told one of my daughters and her husband that their kids were the best-behaved kids she'd seen in her twelve years of flying. She asked the parents how they did it and one of the kids immediately piped up, "We've just gotten manner lessons at Cousin Camp!"

Cousin Camp is definitely making an impression on our grandkids. Last summer, when my granddaughter Morgan was ten, she said, "Nana, I love Cousin Camp! I can't wait till I grow up and have kids of my own and Mom has her own Cousin Camp, because I'm sure I'll need a break from my kids, too."

When I related that to Morgan's mother, a brief look of horror passed over her face, quickly replaced with a knowing nod of the head and a "Thanks a lot, Mom!"

But that at least tells her—and you—that Cousin Camp is well worth the effort.

Final Words of Encouragement

For some of you, the idea of Cousin Camp is natural and pleasant; you picked up this book to supplement your own ideas about how to run such a camp. For others, Cousin Camp seems a daunting and formidable task, something that in your heart of hearts you want to do, but you are fearful that you can't pull it off and that you will come off looking foolish to your own grandchildren. Perhaps you will even damage your relationship with them in some way. You picked up this book to see if indeed the seemingly impossible is somehow doable.

Put those negative thoughts to rest. When you put forth the effort, your grandkids will notice. It doesn't matter if things don't go perfectly according to plan. What matters is that you are spending time with them. They'll recognize that, and that's what they'll remember.

Even if your grandkids are growing up and you don't feel as close to them as you'd like, you can do this. In fact, that's all the more reason to do this.

Equipped with the planning and tools from this book, you can forge stronger relationships with your grandkids. As they grow, you can take on a mentor role, be someone they know, love, and trust to guide them through difficult decisions and to support them in emotionally tough times.

When you are an intentional grandparent, you are taking on a vital role in your grandchildren's lives. You are supplementing the love and support that the children receive in their own home. You are giving the children's parents a much-needed break. You are reinforcing the values that mean so much to you. You are investing your time, love, and energy into one of this world's greatest resources and treasures: children.

I would love to hear from you as you conduct your own camps. Please email me at ramonaroberson@gmail.com with comments, success stories, and suggestions regarding future editions of this book. Be sure to visit my website at: www.ramonaroberson.com.

May God richly bless you as you plan and run your own Cousin Camps!

BREAKFAST
Cereal and toast or Pop-Tarts with banana
French toast with breakfast meat (bacon/sausage)
Scrambled eggs with donuts
Smiley-face or Mickey-Mouse pancakes with syrup (see Appendix B)
Fruit Smoothie (especially good on a hot summer morning) made with fresh fruit and yogurt
Bagels with flavored cream cheese
Omelets in a bag (see Appendix B)

LUNCH
Cold-cut sandwich with chips and fruit
Macaroni and cheese, bread/butter sandwich, cut veggies and ranch dip
Make-your-own pizza with fruit cups
Pizza, Pizza, Pizza (veggie, meat, fruit; see Appendix B)

DINNER
Spaghetti, green salad, toasted French bread
Hamburgers, French fries, cottage cheese
Fish sticks, tater tots, fruit cups
Fried chicken, mixed vegetables, mashed potatoes
Weiner roast: hot dogs, chips, baked beans, s'mores

SNACKS
Milk and cookies in the afternoon (time to burn off sugar before bedtime, milk not good at bedtime for bed-wetters)
 Ice cream sundaes

BEDTIME SNACKS (low sugar and liquids)
Popcorn with frozen grapes (satisfies their thirst w/o a lot of liquids)
Twizzlers
Peach or pear halves with spoon of whipped cream topped with a teddy graham

Smiley-face pancakes:

Spoon pancake batter onto hot griddle in the shape of a smiley face—two drops for the eyes, one drop for the nose, and a smile. Let this cook for 15-20 seconds, then pour batter over the smile to form the complete pancake. Cook as usual. When you flip the pancake, there will be a smiley face on it!

Mickey-Mouse pancakes:

Pouring pancake batter from a spout container, pour out two smaller amounts of batter for the ears, then pour a larger amount below them letting the batter barely touch each other so the pancake is in the shape of Mickey's head. You can drop chocolate chips or blueberries onto the pancake to make a face on it before you flip the pancake.

Babies in a blanket:

Using canned Pillsbury crescent roll dough, cut each triangle of dough into three smaller triangles and wrap them around precooked cocktail weenies, place on cookie sheet and bake according to directions on crescent roll can. Young children love these little babies!

Pizza, Pizza, Pizza:

First Course: Veggie Pizza—Using crescent roll dough, spread into a round crust on a pizza pan and bake. When cool, spread a mixture of cream cheese (thinned out a bit with either ranch dressing or mayonnaise to spreading consistency) over the crust. Chop and cut a variety of vegetables, depending on your children's taste, and spread over crust, creating veggie pizza. (If the veggies are chopped small enough to be unidentifiable, there will be fewer objections from the kids!)

Main Course: Meat or cheese pizza, frozen, homemade or ordered in.

Dessert: Fruit Pizza—Using a can of sugar cookie dough, spread into a crust on a pizza pan making a giant cookie, bake just until lightly golden. (Be careful not to bake too long or it will crumble when you try to cut into slices.) When cookie is cool, spread with vanilla frosting. Thinly slice fruit such as bananas, kiwi, strawberries, and apples and arrange around the top of the pizza. Berries can also be sprinkled on the top. Works best if you can have the fruit ready to go on when you first frost, so it will slightly adhere to the damp frosting before it sets and dries. Helps keep the fruit on the pizza rather than the floor.

Babies in a basket:

Peach halves with a dollop of Cool Whip in the center and a teddy graham cracker stuck in the whipped cream. (You can also use pear halves.)

Omelets in a bag:

Half fill a large saucepan or dutch oven (depending on how many omelets you want to cook at one time) with water and bring to boiling. Have pre-chopped omelet ingredients in separate bowls, such as ham, mushrooms, onions, green peppers to use for the omelet filling. Crack and stir eggs in a mixing bowl with a pour spout. Give each child a zip lock sandwich bag. Let them choose a spoonful of each ingredient they want in their omelet and put them in their zip lock bag; then pour in egg mixture to cover. Close the zip lock bag and drop into boiling water. Takes about three minutes to cook, but you can tell by looking. Using tongs to remove, let cool for a minute, then unzip and slide omelet onto plate.

Jesus' Birthday Cake

Because Christmas is Jesus' birthday, we celebrate it like we would anyone else's. But his birthday cake has special symbolic meaning.

The shape of the cake is round to represent the world into which Jesus was born. Each layer is a different color.

- Bottom layer: Black (chocolate), representing the fact that all men have sinned. This is the reason Jesus came to earth.
- Center layer: Red (strawberry or cherry-flavored with red food coloring), symbolizing Jesus' blood that was shed for our sin.
- Top layer: Green (green coloring) denoting the new life we have in Christ after our sins have been washed away.

The frosting is pure white, standing for the righteousness and purity of Christ.

A border of red hearts stands for brothers and sisters united in Christ circling the earth as his witnesses.

On the top is a gold (or yellow) star typifying the star that shone heralding his birth and lighting the way to where it had taken place. This should be the six-pointed Star of David.

In the center on top is one large red candle representing Jesus who came into the dark world to bring it light and truth.

We gather around the cake and each person is given a small green candle. Grandpa reads the Christmas story out of Luke, or some of the children who have memorized it recite it. Then we light the large red candle and sing happy birthday to Jesus.

After everyone has taken their smaller green candle and lit it from the middle one representing Jesus, they put it in the top of the cake. This represents the fact that we all are to be the light of the world. We sing "Silent Night." Someone prays, thanking God for sending his Son. We blow out the candles and proceed with our Christmas celebration.

APPENDIX C

1. What is today's date? _____

2. How old are you? _____

3. What is your favorite food? _____

4. What is your least favorite food? _____

5. What is your favorite color? _____

6. What is your least favorite color? _____

7. What are your favorite things to do?

_____

_____

_____

8. What are your least favorite things to do?

_____

_____

_____

9. What is your favorite book? _____

10. What is your favorite song? _____

11. Who is your favorite band or singer? _____

12. What is your favorite show? _____

13. Do you like school? _____ Why?

_____

_____

_____

14. Who is your best friend? _____

Why? _____

_____

_____

_____

15. How many brothers do you have? _____
How many sisters? _____

16. What are three things you would like to be when you grow up?

   1.

_____

_____

_____

2.

_____

_____

_____

3.

_____

_____

_____

17. What do you think you will be like in five years?

_____

_____

_____

_____

18. What do you think you will be like in ten years?

_____

_____

_____

_____

APPENDIX D

I (we), the undersigned parent(s) or guardian(s) of _____
_____, _____
_____, a minor(s), do hereby authorize his/
her grandparent(s) for the undersigned, to consent to any medical
or surgical care deemed advisable by any accredited physician or
surgeon in an approved emergency clinic or hospital.

Date signed _____

Parent/Legal Guardian (print) _____

Parent/Legal Guardian (sign)_____

Address _____
City, State_____

Emergency Phone: Home _____
Work_____

Health Insurance Company _____

Policy or Group Number _____
Phone _____

If parent/legal guardian is not available in an emergency,
contact:

Name_____
Phone _____

Please list any allergies, including medications, foods, etc.

_____

_____

Does your child have any medical or special needs, including medications currently being used?

No _____Yes _____If yes, please explain

Doctor's name _____
Phone _____

Dentist's name _____
Phone _____

Date of last tetanus shot _____
Birthdate (s) of Children _____
_____
_____

Check with your local Hospital or Doctor to see if a notarized signature is required.

6016761R0

Made in the USA
Lexington, KY
08 July 2010